German

with a Smile

By HELGA LEES

Illustrations by Rupert Besley

A new dimension to Beginners' German for the post-16 age group and adults in general.

Ideal for the classroom, group tuition or individuals wanting to acquire the language quickly.

COACH HOUSE PUBLICATIONS LTD
The Coach House, School Green Road, Freshwater, Isle of Wight, PO40 9BB
Tel/Fax: 01983 755655

German With a Smile
by H. Lees

Published by:
Coach House Publications Limited

Idea, Test and overall Course Composition

Designed and typeset by H. Lees
Illustrations by Rupert Besley Copyright 1998

Printed in Great Britain
ISBN: 1-899-392-165

A new dimension to Beginners' German for the post-16 age group and adults in general. Ideal for the class-room, group tuition or individuals wanting to acquire the language quickly

Dialogues	**Introducing language useful and relevant to adult learners** from the beginning. Easy guidelines to pronunciation.
Key Phrases	**and core language are shaded and/or marked in bold.**
Vocabulary	**Follows each new text,** key terminology is always shaded. Useful additional vocabulary is contained in the appendix.
Grammar	**A totally positive approach** supported by amusing illustrations. Easily followed explanations of the building blocks of German.
Illustrations	**Depicting situations relevant to real life, within which all the language functions necessary can be practised.** Excellent for vocabulary practice, simulations of conversations, situational dialogues and practising the grammar previously learnt.
Exercises	**To build up the ability to communicate as quickly as possible.** Also to practise the essentials of German grammar in a way which is effective but painless.
Information	**Wide-ranging and useful.** Cultural, business and technical information, contained in the chapters as well as in the appendix.
Appendix	**Valuable reference material** of a general nature plus commercial, business and technical information. Capable of extending the scope of each chapter by using the material as an additional lesson component.

Survival proficiency can be reached in record time. Concentrate on the key dialogues, phrases and core language (shaded and/or bold), within any of the topic areas listed on page 7.

Exam proficiency, through greater in depth study of the course material, will take you from beginners' stage to intermediate exam level (Key Stage 4, GCSE etc.) and beyond in some areas. Practically all exam syllabuses and assessment requirements are catered for.

All the language knowledge you need to function across a wide range of situations is contained here, plus a stimulating and humorous environment, when you want to practise your newly acquired language skills. Easily followed, it tells the story of a young executive, travelling first to Frankfurt, then to Vienna, where he meets a charming student who helps him to cope with the usual travel and social situations.

Fast track, slow route, modular or just for revision, plus useful and relevant material for students with a business or technical background. - this is your ideal study aid!

CONTENT, PICTURES, VOCABULARY, PHRASES, GRAMMAR, APPENDIX

This is a Beginners' Course in German for adults from about 15/16 years of age, who want to get quickly up to standard in learning to use the language effectively or wish to study for any of the examinations and assessments at intermediate level e.g. GCSE (Key Stage 4), GNVQS, Institute of Linguists and various other examinations with a business/commercial/technical bias.

Students are able to study the specific subject areas, topics, listed on p.7, necessary to satisfy all syllabus requirements up to intermediate level, while at the same time covering the theory necessary in a German language course. All along they are working within realistic and useful conversation models.

Course content, key phrases and core vocabulary for survival and exam proficiency are supported by large, lively illustrations relevant to the topics listed. Visual representation i.e. working pictures, are a simulation of reality, they serve as a very effective basis for exercises and a powerful aid for the retention of newly acquired skills.

The course will teach students all the structures and grammar necessary from beginners' stage up to intermediate levels and enable them to function across the topic areas listed by developing all the oral skills necessary.

It should be noted that this approach, i.e. the extensive use of relevant yet amusing illustrations contributes significantly to the effectiveness of the language being taught. These lively and witty pictures will be used in different ways at all stages throughout the course, at beginners' level for vocabulary practice and simple sentences, gradually and painlessly progressing to more complex grammar, structures and oral exercises.

Exercises are only partly prescriptive, mostly when practice of new grammatical elements and structures is called for. However, with the majority of exercises particular emphasis is put on encouraging a free conversational approach, supported, if need be, by recourse to a concise dictionary which should always be readily at hand.

Although there is enough exercise material to practise what is being learnt, there is a great deal more that can be done with the resources contained in this course. Particularly the illustrations can, through imaginative use, be exploited in very many different ways.

Dialogues should ideally either be prepared as homework before or scanned during a lesson before starting work on them. That way students get an idea of the subject matter before them and won't feel too stressed when asked to read or speak.

For a flexible, modular approach individual topics only (i.e. restaurants, shopping etc.) can be worked on separately as modules, concentrating on key phrases (shaded) and core vocabulary (bold/shaded), if time is too short to allow for all the course components to be covered.

The course is held together by a light-hearted story. This in turn is constructed round all the topics (listed on p.7) relevant to the exam requirements at GCSE level. Realistic, real life situations are represented which could easily serve loosely as conversation models to anyone travelling or needing to communicate in German-speaking countries.

John Peters, a young executive travels to Frankfurt where his firm has an office. Subsequently his boss persuades him to come on a weekend visit to Vienna where John encounters all the typical travel and social situations within which students need to function in. There is a slight twist to the story which I leave you to discover.

The reference material plus additional exercises in the appendix, under the relevant headings, increases the usefulness of this book considerably, as all or part of it can be used to extend the teaching content of any of the chapters by cross-referencing. It also provides additional information of value and interest to students from the commercial, business and technical sector.

There are broadly speaking two methods leading to satisfactory proficiency in a foreign language, in this case German. Which way you choose depends on your circumstances, i.e. how much time you have available and what your language needs are.

For quick results concentrate on core vocabulary, key phrases (always shaded or marked in bold) and skeleton grammar only. The language material in this course will provide you with all the essential knowledge to get by, function and communicate across a range of relevant situations in German without fussing too much over grammar. This approach is also successful for basic level exams.

For wide-ranging competence, work step by step, through this foundation course, tailor made for 16 plus / mature students, with or without a teacher, gaining a more thorough understanding of the language and acquiring more profound grammar knowledge leading eventually to all round competence. This will allow students to aim at higher level exams with confidence and enable them to branch out into more specialised fields, something which is often necessary as part of higher education or within the context of industry and commerce, the arts, science or medicine to name but a few.

Whichever approach you envisage, this book will be a very useful companion along the way, its concept being based on sound principles and long experience in conveying foreign language skills.

To help you make rapid progress from the start, the guiding principle behind the creation of this course was to make it as useful, as relevant, effective and 'user friendly' as possible, all in one compact book, which can easily be carried around, while not forgetting that the learning process should also be enjoyable.

Good luck and enjoy yourself !

CONTENTS

Pronunciation 10

CHAPTER 1

Wer ist John Peters? ***Who is John Peters?*** **12**
- John Peters, a young executive, introduces himself. At the office. At the airport.
- *Introductions, phoning, greeting. Welcoming someone, apologising.*
- Articles, present tense, question form, some interrogatives.

CHAPTER 2

Lernen viele Engländer Deutsch? ***Do many British people learn German?*** **21**
- John's boss in Frankfurt talks about his family and enquires if many people in Britain are able to speak German.
- *Talking about family life. Checking in at the airport and a security check.*
- Noun plurals, more interrogatives, stem vowel changes, possessives, 'haben', 'sein'.

CHAPTER 3

Eine kleine Party ***A small party*** **27**
- John meets friends of the Müller family.
- *An invitation, introductions, social interaction,*
- *some food, likes, dislikes.*
- 'nicht', 'kein', adjectives, a gentle introduction to endings.

CHAPTER 4

Wohnen in Deutschland ***Living in Germany*** **32**
- Picture and vocabulary. Topic: 'A German City '.
- *'Verloren? Gestohlen?' (Lost? Stolen?)*
- A gentle start to cases and adjectival endings.
- Word order: Inversion.

CHAPTER 5

Deutschland heute ***Germany today*** **45**
- Picture and vocabulary. Topic: 'A German Landscape'.
- Accusative case and prepositions. Comparative.
- *Am Bahnhof (At the railway station)*

CHAPTER 6

Wien, eine wunderbare Stadt. ***Vienna, a wonderful city*** **56**
- Conversation about life in German towns and Vienna, the capital of Austria.
- *Eine Fahrt mit dem Taxi. (A taxi drive)*
- Superlative, dative case and prepositions, 'können', 'müssen'.
- Word order.

CHAPTER 7

Ein Wochenende in Wien ***A weekend in Vienna*** **63**
- Planning a short holiday in Vienna.
- *Using the phone, booking hotel accommodation in Vienna.*
- Separable verbs, 'sollen', 'wollen', 'möchten' and their effect on word order.
- Making a start on pronouns and their cases.

CHAPTER 8

In Wien ***In Vienna*** **72**
- Was machen wir heute? (What shall we do today?)
- *Beim Frühstück. Einkaufen. Auf der Bank. (At Breakfast. Shopping. At the Bank.)*
- Present tense implying the future, 'dürfen', accusative with direction.
- Prepositions taking dative or accusative. Genitive, genitive prepositions.

CHAPTER 9

Mittagessen mit Sabine ***Lunch with Sabine*** **83**
- John sets out on his own in search of a pleasant restaurant.
- He is soon given friendly advice by a pleasantViennese student.
- *Asking for and giving directions.*
- *The polite way of issuing, accepting or refusing invitations.*
- Imperative, dative verbs, reflexive verbs, 'to', the differences between 'zu' and 'nach'.

CHAPTER 10

Im Restaurant ***At the restaurant*** **92**
- John and Sabine find a nice table in the shade and proceed to order lunch.They are having a really pleasant time.
- *All about ordering and paying for meals.*
- *Introduction to the names of meals and food.*
- Word order, subordinate clauses. Conjunctions: 'daß', 'weil', 'wenn'. Relative pronouns.

CHAPTER 11

Johns charmante Stadtführerin ***John's charming city guide*** **97**

- Sabine, a student at Vienna university, decides exam pressure can be forgotten for the afternoon and agrees to be John's tourist guide. John promises to show her London at some future time.
- *Education, training and qualifications. Jobs and job titles.*
- More subordinate word-order, 'seit' construction.
- Ein schöner Nachmittag. (A pleasant afternoon.)
- *Auf der Post. (At the Post Office.)*

CHAPTER 12

Ein schöner Nachmittag ***A beautiful afternoon*** **104**

- Getting to know 'Apfelstrudel' and 'Eiskaffee' in a Viennese café.
- *Talking about places to go to in the evening. Reserving tickets.*
- *Newspapers, interests, current affairs.*
- The future tense and forms of 'werden', 'würden'.

CHAPTER 13

Eine Verabredung für den Abend ***A date for the evening*** **113**

- John asks Sabine to continue as his tourist guide. Hay-fever strikes.
- *At the chemist. At the doctors.*
- Perfect tense with 'haben'. Formation of past participles. Word order.

CHAPTER 14

John fährt mit der Straßenbahn. ***John takes the tram*** **121**

- He wants to get ready for his evening date with Sabine.
- *Travelling by public transport.*
- The Imperfect. Dative verbs and constructions, 'mögen'. Word order.

CHAPTER 15

Eine große Enttäuschung ***A big disappointment*** **129**

- It is 8 o'clock on a warm summer evening. John has been waiting for well over an hour for Sabine. Why has she not arrived?
- *How to return tickets, cancel arrangements, change bookings and ask for a refund on goods.*
- Pluperfect tense, more imperfect, three ways of expressing 'when'. Relative pronouns.

Topics, key phrases and core language for survival and rôle-play practice

Key phrases in the text as well as core language are always listed separately and shaded.

APPENDIX

Comprehensive supplementary reference source containing a wealth of general back-up information as well as business and technical language. Additional teaching, practice and learning material, which can be drawn on at any stage throughout the course to extend the range of the core language contained in the main text.

German with a Smile

by

Helga Lees

A new dimension to Beginners' German

A BEGINNERS COURSE UP TO GCSE AND BEYOND

PRONUNCIATION

Letter	Sound (Alphabet)	English equivalent	German example
a	**ah**	park, nut	danke, Glas
b	**beh**	same as English	Brot, Butter
c	**tseh**	as in 'cent' before 'e' and 'i'	Celsius
		as in'cat' before 'a','o', 'u'	Café
d	**deh**	same as English	Dahlie
e	**eh**	bed, red, send	Bett, senden
f	**eff**	finger	Finger
g	**geh**	garden, not as in 'general'	Garten
h	**hah**	house	Haus
		silent in the middle	sehen (to see)
		and end of words	Schuh
i	**ee**	in, fill, see	bitte, in
		never as in 'I'	
j	**yot****	young	jung
		never as in 'jetty'	
k	**kah**	coal, cold	Kohle, kalt
l	**ell**	blond	blond

The German 'l' is formed further back in the mouth but an English 'l' sound is quite acceptable.

m	**emm**	same sound	Mutter
n	**enn**	same sound	nein
o	**oh**	not, rob	Brot, rot
		not as in 'most' ['ou' sound]	
p	**peh**	post	Post
qu	**koo**	'kv' sound	Qualität
r	**err**	often guttural (North Germany),	Rest, rollen
		elsewhere rolled or trilled	Dresden
s	**ess**	'z' at the beginning of a word,	Suppe, Sonne
		otherwise as in English	Liste
ß*	**ess tsett****	double 's' sound	er ißt (essen - to eat)
t	**teh**	same sound	Telefon
u	**ooh**	good (not as in 'under')	Hut, gut
v	**fow**	'f' sound, father	Vater
w	**veh**	'v' sound, very	Winter
x	**icks**	same sound	Alexander
y	**ipsilon****	as in 'lyrical',	Physik
z	**tsett**	'ts' as in 'bits'	Zentrum

der Umlaut(e)	a vowel with double dots on	
ä	as in 'care'	Hände (hands)
ö	similar to 'fur'	Söhne (sons)
ü	like 'une' in French	für (for)

* can always be substituted by 'ss'   ** this is the name of the letter, not its sound

au	**ow**	now	braun
äu	**oi**	oil	Häuser (houses)
eu	**oi**	same sound as above	Deutschland
sp	**shp**		Sport
st	**sht**		Sturm
sch	**sh**	shoe	Schuh
ch	**ch**	like 'loch'	ich, nicht
ei	**I**	I, eye, like	Wein, mein
ie	**ee**	see, me	hier, sie
Double vowels		lengthen a syllable	leer (empty)
Double consonants		shorten a syllable	rollen (to roll)

The sound quality of certain vowels and consonants varies considerably throughout the German speaking areas. Even highly educated people, speaking correct standard German which is taught in all schools, will sound different depending on which area they come from. This regional colouring of the sound quality is not to be confused with dialects of which there are many.

Whether German sounds guttural and hard or sing-song and soft, whether spoken fast or slowly, your ability to understand will increase in relation to the amount of exposure to spoken German you can get.

German is a totally phonetic language, once you have learnt the sound values of each letter you can read German. Regarding your own linguistic achievements, be patient and remember that as a child it will have taken you up to two years to learn to speak your own native language even though you were constantly surrounded by and immersed in it. Everyone who has learnt his or her own language is able to learn a foreign language.You just have to give yourself a little time and be as tolerant with yourself as you would be if you tried to teach someone else.

For some time now, there have been moves towards a spelling reform, which should, in theory, be implemented in all German-speaking countries. However, there has been no binding ratification of the proposals, as there are many opponents to the changes who are actively and effectively working against the scheme. It looks as if German is going to be written in its present form for some time yet.

CHAPTER 1

Wer ist John Peters? *Who is John Peters?*

- John Peters, a young executive introduces himself.
- Introductions, greetings, apologies.
- Articles, present tense, question form, some interrogatives.

Shaded or in Bold throughout the Book: All key phrases and vocabulary. Also sentences which could serve as conversation models (substituting different vocabulary or phrase components as necessary, depending on context).

Mein Name ist John Peters, ich bin dreißig Jahre alt.
Ich bin geschieden, leider. Ich komme aus York.
Ich wohne jetzt in London. Mein Büro ist da.
Ich arbeite für eine große Firma, die Firma Elektrona.
Ich lerne Deutsch und spreche oft mit Kollegen in Deutschland.
Meine Firma hat ein Büro in Frankfurt.
Der Chef in Frankfurt ist Herr Müller. Er ist sehr nett.

Meine Sekretärin, Jane, ist jung, attraktiv, verheiratet und auch sehr nett.
Wo finde ich eine nette Partnerin? In Deutschland? In Österreich?
Ich bin oft in Frankfurt und spreche hoffentlich bald gut Deutsch.
Deutsch lernen ist interessant, aber ich habe nie genug Zeit.
Immer viel zu tun. Haben Sie dasselbe Problem?

(Grammar explanations can be found in each chapter, there is also a complete Grammar Survey in the appendix.)

Mein Name ist ...	My name is ...
Ich heiße ...	I am called ...
Guten Tag, guten Morgen	Good day (Hello), good morning
Guten Abend, gute Nacht	Good evening, good night
Auf Wiedersehen!	Good bye!
Auf Wiederhören!	Good bye! (telephone)
Tschüß!	Cheerio!
Hallo!	Hello!
Wie geht's?	How are you?
Wie geht es Ihnen?	(Never used as a greeting, only as a genuine question.)

There are a number of regional variations e.g. **'Grüß Gott' instead of 'Guten Tag'** in Bavaria and Austria, 'Servus' amongst friends in Vienna and 'Grüezi' in Switzerland.

Vocabulary (plural endings in brackets)

das Büro(s)	office	**arbeiten**	to work
der Chef(s)	boss, superior	**finden**	to find
		haben	to have
Deutsch	German (language)	**hat**	has
(das) Deutschland	Germany	**wohnen**	to live
(das) Österreich	Austria	**kommen**	to come
		tun	to do
die Firma(Firmen)	firm, company	**sprechen**	to speak
die Frau(en)	woman, wife, Mrs...	**lernen**	to learn, study
das Fräulein	girl, Miss...		
der Herr(n)	(gentle)man, Mr..		
das Jahr(e)	year		
der Kollege(n)	colleague	**ich**	I
der Name(n)	name	**ich bin**	I am
das Problem(e)	problem	**er/sie**	he/she
die Sekretärin(innen)	secretary	**er/sie ist**	he/she is
die Zeit(en)	time		

alt	old	**aber**	but	**auch**	also
geschieden	divorced	**aus**	from	**bald**	soon
groß	big, tall	**da**	here, there	**für**	for
gut	good				
		in	in	**immer**	always
interessant	interesting	**jetzt**	now	**mit**	with
jung	young	**nie**	never	**oft**	often
nett	pleasant, nice	**sehr**	very	**und**	and
verheiratet	married	**wo**	where	**zu**	to

mein	my	**ein(e)**	a, one
hoffentlich	it is to be hoped	**dreißig**	thirty
leider	unfortunately	**viel/viele**	much/many
(der-, die-)dasselbe	the same		

Single? Married?

ledig	single
(un)verheiratet	(un)married
verlobt	engaged
getrennt	separated
geschieden	divorced
verwitwet	widowed

Ich heiße............................. (Vorname)
Mein Name ist..................(Nachname)
Ich bin................................. Jahre alt.
(Numbers: Appendix, p.147)

Ich bin.................................
Er ist...................................
Sie ist..................................

Turn to the Grammar section at the end of this chapter and find out which ending you need on verbs following **ich, er** and **sie/Sie**. Scan the text on p.1 and use the information to fill the gaps in the following exercises.

Talking about yourself:	Mein Name **i**-- Ich **komm**-- Ich **wohn**-- Ich **arbeit**-- Ich **b**--
Talk about John Peters:	Er **i**-- Er **komm**-- aus Er **wohn**-- jetzt in Er **lern**-- Deutsch. Er **arbeit**-- in (add an 'e' here before the ending)
And what about Jane:	Sie **i**-- **S**---------. Sie **i**-- **j**---. Sie **i**-- **a**--------. Sie **i**-- **n**---. Sie **i**-- **v**----------.
A few questions:	Wo **wohn**-- Sie? Wo **arbeit**-- Sie? Woher **komm**-- Sie? **Lern**-- Sie Spanisch? **Sprech**-- Sie oft Deutsch?

'wo' where, **'woher'** where from, **'ja'** yes, **'nein'** no, **'nicht'** not, **'wie'** how.

Wie alt sind Sie?	Feel free to invent your age! This is not the confessional, we are only practising numbers (Numbers: Appendix, p.147).	
Haben Sie ein Auto?	Wie alt ist das Auto?	(das Auto car)
Haben Sie ein Haus?	Wie alt ist das Haus?	(das Haus house)
Haben Sie eine Wohnung?	Wie alt ist die Wohnung?	(die Wohnung flat)

(A compact, up-to-date dictionary at hand will be very useful.)

- **Am Flughafen Frankfurt** John has arrived at Frankfurt airport.

- **Phoning, greeting and welcoming someone, apologising.**

John: *(Looking round for a phone.)* **Wo ist hier ein Telephon?** Ach, so viele Leute! *(Having waited his turn, dials.)* Firma Elektrona? **John Peters hier. Herr Müller, bitte.**

Sekretärin: **Wie bitte? Herr Müller? Moment, bitte!**

Herr Müller: **Hallo, John? Was ist denn los? Wo sind Sie denn? Wir warten schon. War der Flug verspätet?**

John: Nein, **die Ankunft war pünktlich. Wo ist der Firmenwagen?** Ich warte schon fünfundzwanzig Minuten.

Herr Müller: Ist er noch nicht da? **Entschuldigung!** Eine Panne vielleicht oder ein Stau unterwegs.

John: **Das Beste ist, ich nehme ein Taxi.**

Herr Müller: Nein, das ist nicht nötig, **ich komme sofort!** Kennen Sie mein Auto?

John: Es ist ein Mercedes, silberblau, nicht wahr?

Later at the office in the centre of Frankfurt. John's German colleagues are pleased to see him again.

Colleague: **Willkommen, Herr Kollege! Wie geht's? Bitte nehmen Sie Platz! Eine Tasse Kaffee?**

John: **Vielen Dank, mit Milch und Zucker, bitte.**

- It is the custom to address people with Mr. or Mrs. e.g. 'Herr' und 'Frau Müller', in the workplace, when talking to neighbours, acquaintances, older people etc. Although eventually progressing to Christian name terms is quite often the case, it is absolutely essential to wait until one is invited to do so.

Entschuldigung!	Apologies!	**Was ist los?**	What is the matter?
Entschuldigen Sie, bitte!	Excuse me, please!	**Wo sind Sie?**	Where are you?
Es tut mir (sehr) leid!	I am sorry!	**Wie bitte?**	Pardon?
Verzeihung!	I am sorry!	**Nicht wahr?**	Isn't it?
Bitte, nehmen Sie Platz!	Please, take a seat!	**Vielen Dank!**	Many thanks

die Ankunft(¨e)	arrival
das Auto(s)	car
das Beste	the best
der Dank	thanks
Vielen Dank!	many thanks
der Firmenwagen(¨)	company-car
der Flug(¨e)	flight
der Kaffee(s)	coffee
die Leute	people
die Milch	milk
die Minute(n)	minute
die Panne(n)	breakdown (car)
der Stau(s)	traffic jam
die Tasse(n)	cup
das Taxi(s)	taxi
das Telephon(e)	telephone
der Zucker(-)	sugar

kennen	to know
nehmen	to take
war	was
warten	to wait
blau	blue
nötig	necessary
silber	silver
pünktlich	on time
unterwegs	en route
verspätet	late
vielleicht	perhaps
willkommen	welcome

nicht	not
noch nicht	not yet
schon	already
sofort	straight away

denn	then
hier	here
oder	or
was	what

Rôle Play:

Imagine, someone you have not seen for a while has just arrived. Work in a group or in pairs if possible. Don't be shy! Shake hands! However, while you are concentrating on what you want to say, don't forget to let go of the other person's hand! Contrary to popular belief it is not customary for men to click heels! A slight bow of the head is considered polite though.

When working through exercises like the one below it is always useful to make a few notes, jot down your answers in rough, practise (quietly) before attempting to speak.
Your teacher will practise difficult words with the whole group as often as it takes to get the pronunciation right.

Exercises:

Greet him/her:
Welcome him/her:
Say, you have been waiting 'x' number of minutes: (use present tense)
Ask what the matter was:
Was the flight late?
Ask how he/she is:
Ask him/her to take a seat:

GRAMMAR NOTES

A summary of all the grammar dealt with in the text can be found in the Appendix.

The Article

The definite article 'the' and the indefinite article 'a'.

		der (m.)	der Elefant, der Garten, der Mann
the	can be	**die (f.)**	die Hand, die Rose, die Frau
		das (n.)	das Buch, das Glas, das Kind

'der' is called the 'masculine', 'die' the 'feminine' and 'das' the 'neuter' article.

		ein (m.)	ein Elefant, ein Garten, ein Mann
'a'	can be	**eine (f.)**	eine Hand, eine Rose, eine Frau
		ein (n.)	ein Buch, ein Glas, ein Kind

'the' in the plural is fortunately just one word: 'die' as in 'die Gärten', 'die Männer'.

There is often an 'Umlaut' in the plural e.g. 'der Garten', 'die Gärten'.
In the vocabulary this is shown in brackets along with the plural ending.

Nouns: always one of three 'genders': masculine (m.), feminine (f.) or 'neuter' (n.).
They always begin with a capital letter in German.

As you learn your vocabulary, you will gradually remember whether a noun is masculine, feminine or neuter. If you don't, it does not make much difference as far as making yourself understood. Whether you say e.g. 'der', 'die' or 'das Garten' does not really matter all that much as everyone will understand the 'Garten' bit.

Have you been traumatised for life by your experiences with grammar at school? Lots of people have, so you are not alone. Most probably inappropriate teaching and/or your attitude at the time will have been the likely factors to have resulted in your dislike of anything to do with 'Grammar'.

Forget the past, this is a new beginning! You need to know the basics of German Grammar to make sense of the language. That does not mean you have to grasp everything the first time it is mentioned, just go with the flow, things will naturally fall into place later on.

The emphasis of this course is to learn to use the spoken language as much as possible. You will always be encouraged to express yourself, to communicate at all costs, grammar mistakes or not.

There will be ample opportunity to practise grammar for those students wanting to study the language thoroughly and/or pass an exam at intermediate level after completing this foundation course. This can be done not only by working through conventional exercises but also through the medium of the subject-related pictures found in this book.

This picture-related approach is very much appreciated by adult students. It is fun as well as being very effective, as practically all actions representing everyday life situations are covered. Young learners always respond to pictures with great enthusiasm, adults even more so, since good, funny graphics never seem to feature much in adult textbooks.

It is hoped that you get some enjoyment from looking at the pictures when you want to practise the language in some way, perhaps by trying to just practise vocabulary to start off with.

Noun practice

Look at the picture of life in a German city and find five examples of nouns for each gender, write them down in three separate blocks.

Verbs in German have more endings than in English, where only the 'he', 'she' ,'it' form requires an 's' ending e.g. 'I come' but 'he', 'she', 'it comes', all other forms like 'you', 'we', 'they come', remain unchanged.

The Present Tense

kommen to come

This, the basic form of the verb, is called the Infinitive.

Take away the ending -en and add whichever ending you need, using the ones below.

singular (re. one person or thing)		plural (re. several persons or things)	
ich komm**e**	I come (am coming)	wir komm**en**	we come (are coming)
du komm**st**	you come (are coming)	ihr komm**t**	you come (are coming)
Sie komm**en**	you come (polite form)	Sie komm**en**	you come (polite form)
er	he		
sie komm**t**	she comes (is coming)	sie komm**en**	they come (are coming)
es	it		

Verbs with stems ending in 't' or 'd' like war**t**en (to wait), arbei**t**en (to work), fin**d**en (to find) or sen**d**en (to send) **need an -et ending instead of just a -t** in the 'er', 'sie', 'es' form e.g. er wart**et**, er find**et**. This helps to make pronunciation easier.

There are no -ing forms in German, the continuity of an action is expressed by the simple verb form only e.g. 'Ich komme jetzt' means 'I am coming now'.

This sometimes accounts for the fact that Germans seem to sound abrupt when they are speaking English as 'I come now' would to them be a natural translation from German as they have no equivalent to 'I am coming now'.

Verb endings are confusing at first and best learnt by heart if you want to express yourself correctly. Don't expect to remember them immediately, get a feeling of the language first, try to remember basic vocabulary and phrases then work on the details.

If the right ending does not come to mind immediately and thinking about it would interrupt a conversation just use the -en form of whichever verb you are just using.

Whether you say 'ich kommen' (wrong) instead of 'ich komme' (correct) will hardly be noticed in a conversation and everybody will know you are not talking about anything other than 'to come'. As a beginner you are bound to make mistakes here and there, don't let that fact stop you from speaking and communicating.

Exercise:

Present tense practice

Write down the complete forms of	wohnen	to live
	kennen	to know
	lernen	to learn
	warten	to wait (see above)

Sie	you (polite)	Used when addressing adults, always, unless invited to use 'Du'.
Du	you (familiar)	Means you are now on Christian name terms. Always used with very good friends, children and animals e.g. pets.

Questions: Simply start with the verb.

Question: Wohnt John in London?
Answer: Ja, er wohnt in London.

Question: Lernt er Spanisch?
Answer: Nein, er lernt Deutsch.

There is no 'do you....', 'does he....', 'do we....'? etc.
Just 'lives he....'?, 'learns John....'?
with the stress on the first word, the verb, e.g. 'wohnt er....'?, 'lernt John....'?

CHAPTER 2

Lernen viele Engländer Deutsch?
Do many British people learn German?

- John's boss in Frankfurt talks about his family and enquires if many people in Britain are able to speak German.

- Checking in at the airport and a security check.

- Noun plurals, more interrogatives, stem vowel changes, possessives, 'haben', 'sein'.

Herr Müller: **John Peters ist ein Kollege aus England,** er kommt oft nach Frankfurt.
Wir finden John sehr sympathisch.

Meine Frau ist Sekretärin, aber nur halbtags. Das ist besser für unsere Familie.

Wir haben zwei Kinder. Paul, unser Sohn, ist achtzehn Jahre alt. Katrin, unsere Tochter, ist sechzehn.

Beide lernen Englisch und sprechen recht gut. Sie hören Englisch im Radio und sehen oft englische oder amerikanische Filme. Sie finden auch Popsongs aus England und Amerika sehr gut.

Sprechen viele Leute in England Deutsch?

John: **Nein, leider nicht.** Viele Kinder lernen Französisch, nur manche lernen Deutsch.

Herr Müller: Deutsch ist doch wichtig, finden Sie nicht?

John: Ja, natürlich. Man spricht auch in Osteuropa und Rußland mehr Deutsch als Englisch.

Herr Müller: **Hier ist Englisch sehr populär.** Junge Deutsche sprechen meist gut Englisch.

John: Deutsch ist schwer für uns. **Ich konzentriere mich auf Sprechen und Verstehen.** Sehr viele deutsche und englische Wörter sind ähnlich.

Englisch	English (lang.)	**Französisch**	French (lang.)
englisch	English	**französisch**	French
England	England	**Frankreich**	France
Amerika	America	**Rußland**	Russia
amerikanisch	American	**russisch**	Russian
Europa	Europe	**Osteuropa**	Eastern Europe
der/die Deutsche(n)	German (person)	**deutsch**	German

die Familie(n)	family	**der Popsong(s)**	pop song
der Sohn(¨e)	son	**das Radio(s)**	radio
die Tochter(¨)	daughter	**das Wort(¨er)**	word
ähnlich	similar	**zwei**	two
besser	better	**achtzehn**	eighteen
halbtags	half a day	**sechzehn**	sixteen
meist	mostly	**manche**	some (countable)
leider	unfortunately		
schwer	difficult	**sehen**	to see
sympathisch	likable, nice	**konzentrieren**	to concentrate
wichtig	important	**verstehen**	to understand
		(Used like nouns, verbs too start with	
mehr...als	more...than	capitals. See prevous page.)	
auch	also	**ganz**	quite
doch	indeed	**im**	in (the)
für	for	**man**	one (e.g. one has..)
nach (Frankfurt)	to	**so viele**	so many
nur	only	**recht**	quite
wir	we	**sind**	are

'wie' how, what like, **'warum'** why, **'wie viel'** how much, **'wie viele'** how many, **'was'** what, **'wo'** where, **'wer'** who.

Wer ist Herr Müller?
Was ist Frau Müller?
Wie viele Kinder haben Herr und Frau Müller?
Wo ist Englisch sehr populär?
Was lernen viele Kinder in England?
Finden Sie Deutsch schwer?

Wer ist Jane?
Wie lang arbeitet sie?
Lernen die Kinder Spanisch?
Was hören die Kinder oft?
Was sprechen die Leute in England?
Wo spricht man auch Deutsch?
Wer ist sympathisch?

Now read through the dialogue again, look away and try to tell the story again in short, simple sentences. To start with you will only remember a few words at a time, gradually however, your memory will cope with more words. It also helps a lot to practise vocabulary and pronunciation by reading and re-reading aloud the texts you have previously gone through.

- **Die Familie**

der Vater(¨)	father	**der Mann(¨er)**	man, husband, Mr.
die Mutter(¨)	mother	**die Frau(en)**	woman, wife, Mrs.
der Bruder(¨)	brother	**die Schwester(n)**	sister
der Sohn(¨e)	son	**die Tochter(¨)**	daughter
die Geschwister	siblings	**Schwiegermutter**	mother in law
die Zwillinge	twins	**Schwiegervater**	father in law
das Kind(er)	child		

Exercise:

Haben Sie Geschwister? Wie heißen sie?
Wie alt ist Ihr Bruder, Ihre Schwester?
Wie alt ist Ihr Mann, Ihre Frau, Ihr Partner, Ihre Partnerin?
Wie alt ist Ihr Sohn, Ihre Tochter, Ihr Hund, Ihre Katze?
(Feel free to invent the ages of the people above, we are practising numbers.)
Possessive adjectives (see below and next page) will be required for this exercise.

Possessive adjectives

der Hund(e) **m.*** dog — **mein** Hund, **Ihr** Hund, (**ein** Hund)

As is the case with 'ein', there is a feminine ending on 'Ihr', 'mein' and all other possessives before feminine nouns:

die Katze(n) **f.*** cat — **meine** Katze, **Ihre** Katze, (**eine** Katze)

***The noun following the possessive adjective determines its gender and ending.**
('mein Hund' but 'meine Katze')

Exercises: Group or pair work. Ask one another the following questions.

Ist Ihre Frau/Partnerin/Schwester/Tochter etc. Sekretärin, Hausfrau etc.?
Was ist Ihr Mann/Partner/Bruder/Sohn? (Appendix: 'Jobs'/'Professions' p.168-170)
Imagine you are showing photos to German friends. Translate into German:
This is my father, his dog and cat. Our mother and her sister.
Their house and their car. Here is our office in London.

sein	to be			
ich bin	I am	**wir sind**	we are	Sie sind.... You are....
du bist	you are (f.)	**ihr seid**	you are	Sind Sie...? Are you...?
Sie sind	you are (p.)	**Sie sind**	you are	We will be using the 'Sie' form mainly, as the conversations are between adults.
er	he			
sie ist	she is	**sie sind**	they are	
es	it			

(f.) - familiar form
(p.) - polite form
These will not be marked separately from now on. See Grammar, chapter 1, 'Du', 'Sie'.

haben	**to have**		
ich habe	I have	**wir haben**	we have
du hast	you have	**ihr habt**	you have
Sie haben	you have	**Sie haben**	you have
er	he		
sie hat	she has	**sie haben**	they have
es	it		

Vowel changes in the 'du' and 'er', 'sie', 'es' form of verbs are quite common, you will learn about them as we go along. See also: List of irregular verbs p.200, second column.

sprechen	ich spreche	There is no change
	Sie sprechen	in the plural forms.
	du sprichst	
	er	
	sie spricht	
	es	

Possessive adjectives

sg.						pl.				
mein	**dein**	**Ihr**	**sein**	**ihr**	**sein**	**unser**	**euer**	**Ihr**	**ihr**	f. familiar
my	your f.	your p.	his	her	its	our	your f.	your p.	their	p. polite

- **Am Flughafen** — At the airport
- **Einchecken** — Checking in
- **Possessive adjectives** (see pages 23 and 24)

John: *(putting his passport and ticket on the counter and placing his case on the conveyor belt)*
Mein Paß, mein Flugschein. Ist mein Koffer zu schwer?

Lady: **Nein, alles ist in Ordnung. Raucher oder Nichtraucher?**

John: **Nichtraucher, bitte.**

Lady: **Ihre Bordkarte. Flugsteig 12, ab 1 Uhr.**

(Having passed through passport control John is about to take his hand-luggage after it had been X-rayed. Two officials approach him.)

Official: Bitte, kommen Sie herüber! Ist das Ihre Reisetasche?

John: Ja, warum?

Official: Einen Moment, und dieser Koffer?

John: *(impatiently)* Ja, das ist mein Aktenkoffer und das ist meine Reisetasche.
Was ist denn los?

Official: Bitte öffnen Sie beide Gepäckstücke!

John: *(getting agitated)* Bitte, meine Herrn, ich habe nicht viel Zeit! Mein Flug ist in zwanzig Minuten!

Official: *(not taking any notice)* Bitte nehmen Sie alles heraus!

John: Mein Pyjama, meine Unterwäsche, mein Deutschbuch, meine Socken, was denn noch?

Official: Was haben Sie denn hier? *(pointing at some small boxes at the bottom of his travel bag)*

John: Das sind harmlose elektronische Bauteile, Muster für unsere Kunden in Deutschland. Ich arbeite für die Firma Elektrona, hier ist meine Karte.

- The following vocabulary list contains additional vocabulary re.'Airports', 'Flying'.

die Ankunft(¨e)	arrival	**das Flugzeug(e)**	aeroplane
die Abfertigung(en)	departure	**der Flugsteig(e)**	departure gate
		der Flughafen(¨)	airport
das Fließband(¨er)	conveyor-belt	**fliegen**	to fly
der Kofferkuli(s)	trolley		
		(Nicht)Raucher	(non)smoker
der Zoll	customs	**rauchen**	to smoke
verzollen	to declare	**öffnen**	to open
zollfrei	duty-free		
der Kunde(n)	customer	**das Bauteil(e)**	component, element
		das Muster(-)	sample (also pattern)
der Aktenkoffer(-)	attaché case	**die Bordkarte(n)**	boarding pass
die Brieftasche(n)	wallet	**der Flugschein(e)**	ticket
das Gepäckstück(e)	item of luggage	**das Ticket(s)**	ticket
das Handgepäck	hand-luggage	**die Karte(n)**	(business)card
der Koffer(-)	suit-case	**der Paß(¨sse)**	passport
die Reisetasche(n)	travel-bag	**das Scheckbuch(¨er)**	cheque-book
Einen Moment!	One moment!	**Was noch?**	What else?
Meine Herrn!	Gentlemen!	**Alles ist in Ordnung!**	Everything is okay
das Buch(¨er)	book	**die Unterwäsche**	underwear
die Socke(n)	sock	**der Pyjama(s)**	pyjamas
elektronisch	electronic	**harmlos**	harmless
schwer	heavy		
ab	from	**dieser(e, es)**	this
heraus (hinaus)	out	**herüber (hinüber)**	over here

her- and **hin-** denote direction
her- towards the speaker **hin-** away from the speaker

The Plural of Articles and Nouns:

'the' in the plural has only one equivalent: 'die' (for all three genders)

Noun endings vary in the plural, they can be -e, -en, -n, -er, -er, -s or no ending.

Very often there is an 'Umlaut' (¨): 'der Vater' but 'die Väter'

CHAPTER 3

Eine kleine Party *A small party*

- John meets friends of the Müller family.
- An invitation, introductions, social interaction, food, likes, dislikes.
- 'nicht', 'kein', adjectives (a gentle introduction to endings)

Herr Müller: **John, haben Sie heute abend Zeit? Darf ich Sie einladen?** Ein paar gute Bekannte kommen zu uns. Kommen Sie auch?

John: **Danke für die Einladung, ich komme gern.** Wann beginnt die Party?

Herr Müller: Um acht Uhr.

(later)

Herr Müller: **Guten Abend, John, bitte kommen Sie herein!** Hier sind einige gute Freunde! **Darf ich vorstellen?** John, mein Kollege aus England.

Party guest: **Mein Name ist Klaus. Klaus Schmitt und das ist meine Frau Jutta.**
Willkommen in Frankfurt! Es ist schön sie hier in Deutschland zu begrüßen.
(Sehr) **angenehm, sehr erfreut.** *(Handshakes all round)*

Exercise:	Practise introducing yourself. Work in pairs or groups.

Klaus: Wie lang bleiben Sie denn hier?

John: Nicht lang genug, nur eine oder zwei Wochen, leider.

Herr Müller: **Ein Glas Wein? Weißwein, Rotwein, Bier, Mineralwasser?**

John: **Ein Glas Weißwein, bitte, kein Bier, danke.**

Herr Müller: **Hier ist Ihr Glas Wein, John. Etwas zu essen?** Belegte Brötchen mit Schinken, Wurst und Käse? Etwas zum Knabbern? Nüsse, Chips, Käsestäbchen? Vielleicht Salzstangen, Bretzel oder Oliven.

John: **Danke schön** *(taking some food)*.

Klaus:	Sie sprechen sehr gut Deutsch. Wo lernen Sie die Sprache?
John:	Ich lerne im Abendkurs, Deutsch und Spanisch. Mein Deutsch ist leider noch lange nicht perfekt Aber es ist besser als nichts.
Klaus:	Das ist richtig.

Bitte kommen Sie herein!	Please, come in!
Darf ich Sie einladen?	May I invite you?
Heute Abend.	This evening. (Expressions of time, p.148)
Darf ich vorstellen?	May I introduce?
'sehr erfreut' or **'sehr angenehm' (*)**	I am very happy (to meet you)

Germans like to be introduced quite promptly, alternatively they will introduce themselves by telling you their names as they shake hands with you.You are then expected to say: (see *) and give them your name.

(das ist) richtig or **(das) stimmt**	(that) is right, correct
Wann beginnt die Party?	When does the party start?
Um acht Uhr.	At eight o'clock. (Times of the clock, p.147)
die Einladung(en)	invitation

der Abend(e)	evening		
der Abendkurs(e)	evening class	**begrüßen**	to greet, welcome
die Sprache(n)	language	**bleiben**	to stay
		danken	to thank
der/die Bekannte(n)	friend, acquaintance	**essen**	to eat
der Freund(e)	(close) friend (masc.)	**einladen**	to invite
die Freundin(nen)	(close) friend (fem.)	**knabbern**	nibble
		vorstellen	to introduce
das Glas(¨er)	glas	**das Bretzel(-)**	pretzel
das Bier(e)	beer	**Chips**	crisps
das Brot(e)	bread	**die Nuß(¨e)**	nut
(belegte Brote	open sandwiches)	**die Olive(n)**	olive
das Mineralwasser	mineral water	**die Salzstange(n)**	salty bread stick
der Wein(e)	wine	**das Stäbchen (Käsestäbchen)**	stick
der Rotwein(e)	red wine		
der Weißwein(e)	white wine	**der Schinken(-)**	ham
der Käse(-)	cheese	**die Wurst(¨e)**	sausage
danke(schön)	thank you (very much)	**gern**	certainly, with pleasure

besser als nichts	better than nothing	**ein paar**	a few
Wie lang?	How long?	**einige**	some, a few (e.g. nuts)
Wann?	When?	**etwas**	some (e.g. salt)
heute	today	**schön**	nice, beautiful
denn	then (filler word)	**zu uns**	to us

How to use 'kein':

ein a, one **kein** no (not a.........)
Ist hier ein Park? Nein, hier ist kein Park. (Preferable to 'nicht ein Park'.)
Ein Haus aber kein Garten. A house but no garden.

Rôle Play: Use the previous text as a basis for rôle play, work in pairs or groups.
Invite someone to come to a party.
Thank him/her, accept the invitation.
When does the party start?
Introduce yourself and respond to someone being introduced to you.
Ask, how long someone is staying.
Offer something to drink. Say, you like beer but no wine for you.
Offer something to eat.

'gern'/'nichtgern' after a verb indicates **liking/not liking** what the verb stands for.
Ich **esse gern** Oliven. Ich **trinke gern** Wein.
Ich **esse nicht gern** Fisch. Ich **trinke nicht gern** Schnaps.

Was essen Sie gern/nicht gern?
Was trinken Sie gern/nicht gern?
Imagine, you are preparing for a party. Make a list of items. Work in groups or pairs. (See 'Food', p.152-157 to help you with the exercises above.)

'nicht' (not)	**Kommen Sie?** Are you coming?	**Nein, ich komme nicht.** No, I am not coming.

When invited, always bring either flowers or chocolates or both but not bottles of wine. You may be tempted to say: 'Wie geht's?' when meeting people. As it is always a genuine question you can only use the phrase if you know the person. If this is indeed the case be prepared to hear all the news, good and bad, including summaries of recent medical events, family troubles or otherwise etc., etc. Foreigners new to Britain are always amazed to be asked by total strangers, how they are, only to be quickly cast aside without having time to answer.

- **John is asked about life in England**

German people are always very interested to find out about other peoples' countries, living standards, politics, current affairs etc. They are usually well informed and don't consider it impolite to ask searching questions or express their own opinions.

- Conversation about houses, flats, cars, gardens, plants etc. Key phrases.

Klaus: **Herr Peters, Sie kommen aus Südengland. Haben Sie dort ein Haus?**

John: **Nein, ich habe eine Wohnung in London.** Meine Eltern haben ein Haus in der Nähe von Chichester.

Klaus: **Wie ist die Stadt? Ist sie groß? Gibt es dort viel Industrie?**

John: Nein, die Stadt ist nicht sehr groß, aber historisch interessant. **Es gibt dort viele alte Häuser und eine gotische Kathedrale.** Hier ist ein Photo von Chichester, das ist unser Haus.

Jutta Ach, wie hübsch! **Typisch englisch,** meinst Du nicht auch, Klaus?

Klaus: **Ja, der Garten vorn und hinten, der perfekte Rasen, und die schönen Blumenbeete rechts und links.**

John: **Es gibt auch ein paar Bäume und Ziersträucher.**

Exercise:	Haben Sie ein Haus oder eine Wohnung? (House and Home: p.158 - 168) Ist da auch ein Garten? Was gibt es da? (Da ist ..., da sind ...) Welche Pflanzen finden Sie schön? ('welche' which) See also 'House' (p.158) and 'Plants and Flowers' (p.161).

John: **Da ist die Garage, links. Das ist mein Auto davor. Rechts ist der Schuppen, dahinter ist ein Teich und ein Gartenhaus.**

Jutta: Das ist ja ein Jaguar Sportwagen, Typ E, toll!

John: Er ist sehr alt und Reparaturen sind immer teuer.

Jutta: Wie ist denn das Klima in England?

John:	Im Süden relativ mild.
Jutta:	Das ist gut für die Pflanzen. **Arbeiten Sie gern im Garten?**
John:	**Nein, nicht sehr,** aber ich helfe manchmal. **Meine Eltern haben mehr Zeit, sie sind im Ruhestand.**
Klaus:	**Gartenarbeit ist für viele Engländer ein Hobby, nicht wahr?**
John:	Richtig.

Exercise:	Haben Sie ein Auto? Ist das Auto ein Jaguar? Haben Sie oft Reparaturen? Sind Sie im Ruhestand?

die Stadt(¨e)	town, city	**das Auto**	car
das Haus(¨er)	house	**die Garage(n)**	garage
die Wohnung(en)	flat	**die Reparatur(en)**	repair
die Kathedrale(n)	cathedral		
(der Dom	cathedral)	**das Klima**	climate
die Industrie(n)	industry	**der Süden**	the South
der Garten(¨)	garden	**das Gartenhaus(¨er)**	summer house
die Pflanze(n)	plant	**der Schuppen(-)**	shed
der Baum(¨e)	tree	**der Rasen(-)**	lawn
die Blume(n)	flower	**der Teich(e)**	pond
das Blumenbeet(e)	flower bed		
der Strauch(¨er)	bush	**die Arbeit(en)**	work
(Zierstrauch	ornamental bush)	**das Hobby(s)**	hobby

alt	old	**der Ruhestand**	retirement
links	left, to the left	**die Eltern**	parents
rechts	right, to the right	**das Photo(s)**	photo
vorn	at the front		
hinten	at the back		
in der Nähe	near	**es gibt**	there is/are
		helfen	to help
manchmal	sometimes	**meinen**	to think (opinion)
ziemlich	rather, fairly		

CHAPTER 4

Wohnen in Deutschland *Living in Germany*

- Picture and vocabulary. Topic: 'A German City '.
  (For practice in all the skills areas taught throughout the book, all levels).
- A gentle start to cases and adjectival endings.
- Word order: Inversion.

Herr Müller: *(looking at John's photos)* **Das ist ein schönes Haus und ein großer Garten.** In Deutschland kostet so etwas viel Geld.

John: Ich glaube, Baukosten sind höher. Aber **Sie haben eine sehr gemütliche Wohnung hier.** Wohnen Sie gern in Frankfurt?

Herr Müller: Doch, **wir wohnen hier sehr gern.** Frankfurt ist eine große, moderne Stadt, das Finanzzentrum Deutschlands.

John: Da ist immer viel los. Viel Verkehr, viele Geschäfte, viele Menschen.

Herr Müller: Natürlich gibt es auch genug Probleme: Arbeitslosigkeit,Wohnungsnot, Drogen, die enorme Zuwanderung von Ausländern und ihre Integration.

Exercise:	Ist Frankfurt eine kleine Stadt? Sind Häuser in Deutschland billig? Hat die Stadt Probleme? Gibt es Probleme, wo Sie wohnen?

John: **Haben viele Leute Häuser in Deutschland?** (see p.153)

Herr Müller: **Nein, die meisten Deutschen wohnen in Wohnungen.** Es gibt Eigentumswohnungen, Mietwohnungen, Sozialwohnungen u.s.w.

John: Kaufpreise für Häuser in Großbritannien sind leider auch ein großes Problem. Viele Engländer kaufen oder mieten deshalb Wohnungen. Meist arbeiten beide Partner, da ist nie genug Zeit für Gartenarbeit, also ist eine Wohnung besser.

Herr Müller: **Ist Ihre Wohnung weit vom Zentrum Londons?** Denn in London zu parken ist ja fast unmöglich.

John: **Ja, meine Wohnung ist sehr zentral gelegen**, das ist ein großer Vorteil.
Meist gehe ich zu Fuß oder nehme die Untergrundbahn.

Mein Auto habe ich für das Wochenende und längere Fahrten.

Herr Müller: Haben Sie eine große Wohnung?

John: Nein, sie ist nur klein aber groß genug.

(Information on the types of houses and flats found in Germany, Austria etc. can be found in the appendix, p.158-161)

Exercise:	Wohnen Sie gern in ...... ? Was ist besser, ein Haus oder eine Wohnung? Ist es besser ein Haus/eine Wohnung zu mieten oder zu kaufen? Gehen Sie oft zu Fuß? ('gehen' to go, 'fahren' to drive)

Hints to the individual student working on his own:

As learning to communicate actively i.e. asking and responding to questions as well as listening to and expressing opinions is central to the aims of this course there will be plenty of opportunity to do just that in exercises like the ones above.

There are a variety of excellent tapes available to teach you the sounds and pronunciation of the German language, listening to these and the many German-speaking channels on Satellite-TV will make your task much easier and more enjoyable.

When attempting the question and answer exercises you will have to pretend you are two people having a conversation. Give yourself time to work out the answers, make rough notes and then, well prepared, engage yourself in conversation! If there is time, tape yourself to check pronunciation.

Using the course in a class-room or group context:

Students should be encouraged to use simple straightforward sentences based mainly on the material learnt already. Use of a dictionary is fine as people will want to refer to their individual circumstances.

Grammar plays only a supporting role here, making oneself understood is the prime purpose of the exercises like the ones we have seen in this chapter and before.

However, good pronunciation is important and should patiently be worked on, as often and for as long as necessary.

Teacher and fellow students should always be ready to help the speaker along and keep up the momentum of the conversation. This approach will avoid long pregnant pauses if the student gets stuck. It is essential to allow a little time to prepare and practise answers and to make rough notes.

die Baukosten	building-costs	**der Mensch(en)**	human being
das Geld(er)	money		
der Kaufpreis(e)	purchase-price		
das Geschäft(e)	shop	**glauben**	to believe
die Fahrt(en)	trip	**parken**	to park
der Verkehr	traffic	**fahren**	to drive
die Untergrundbahn	underground		
(U-Bahn)	train	**gehen**	to go, walk
das Wochenende(-)	week-end	**zu Fuß gehen**	to walk
der Vorteil(e)	advantage	**kaufen**	to buy
der Nachteil(e)	disadvantage	**mieten**	to rent
		kosten	to cost

die Eigentumswohnung(en)	privately owned apartment
die Mietwohnung(en)	rented apartment
die Sozialwohnung(en)	municipal flat

Owning property in Germany is not as wide-spread as in Britain, a lot of people rent flats and are proud to do so. They very often spend a lifetime in their rented flats and regard them on the whole as a long-term solution, willing to invest plenty of money on improving their accommodation.

der Ausländer(-)	foreigner (male)	**die Droge(n)**	drug
die Ausländerin(nen)	foreigner(female)	**die Zuwanderung**	immigration
die Arbeitslosigkeit	unemployment	**die Wohnungsnot**	lack of accomodation

gemütlich	comfortable, cosy	**also**	well, therefore (filler word)
höher	higher		
hoch	high	**denn**	because
klein	small	**deshalb**	therefore
groß	big	**doch**	yes, indeed
länger	longer		
lang	long	**fast**	almost
modern	modern	**ja**	isn't it? (often used to emphasise a point)
(un)möglich	(im)possible		
weit	far	**noch**	still
zentral gelegen	centrally situated	**u.s.w.** (und so weiter	etc. and so on)

Word order:	**2** Beide Partner **arbeiten** meist. Word order as in English. However, when you start with e.g. 'meist', the verb follows: **2** Meist **arbeiten** beide Partner. This is called 'Inversion'
Inversion:	**In a Main Clause i.e. a statement, the verb is always the second element.**

Exercises:

Look for examples of inversion in the preceding dialogue.

Rewrite the following sentences starting with 'jetzt' (now, nowadays)
Eine Wohnung ist besser als ein Haus. Jetzt **ist** eine Wohnung besser als ein Haus.
Viele Leute haben nicht viel Zeit.
Ich bin noch Student.
Baukosten sind höher in Deutschland.
Ich habe mein Auto für das Wochenende.

Whether you get this aspect of German word-order right or wrong makes little difference. Don't worry at this stage! As a Beginner it is important to concentrate on conveying the meaning of what you wish to say.

You will be understood whether you say: 'Jetzt eine Wohnung ist besser als ein Haus' (incorrect, the verb here is the third element) or 'Jetzt ist eine Wohnung besser als ein Haus (correct, the verb is the second element) Later on, if you want to pass exams at higher levels, these things start to matter more. For now, spoken communication is all!

On a general note, it is important not to get too perfectionist at this stage at trying to use absolutely correctly all the material learnt. It is early days yet, have patience! After all, learning to drive does not immediately make you into a racing driver but it gets you from A to B without having to walk. The same principle applies to learning a language. A little German will go far if you refuse to be shy about using it.

Endings: You will have noticed a variation in endings on adjectives, words qualifying the noun i.e. instead of 'der groß Garten', it is 'der groß**e** Garten'. These endings depend on the gender (and a number of other things which will be explained later). As they are unstressed it will go largely unnoticed whether you have used the right one or not.

The Nominative

sg.			pl.
m.	f.	n.	all genders
der groß**e** Garten	die groß**e** Stadt	das groß**e** Haus	die groß**en** Häuser
ein groß**er** Garten	eine groß**e** Stadt	ein groß**es** Haus	keine groß**en** Häuser

The possessive adjectives: 'mein', 'dein' etc. follow the same pattern as 'ein' and 'kein'.
'Mein groß**er** Garten'... etc.

Look back into the previous dialogue and find examples of adjectives and nouns showing the changes explained above.
Choose five nouns for each gender from one of the pictures and write them down in three blocks (one for masculine, one for feminine and one for neuter). Team them up with different adjectives (supplied in the list of topic vocabulary supplied with the pictures), allowing for the changes discussed above. Vary the articles. Don't forget that the gender of the noun determines the ending on the adjective.
Good hunting!

The picture and related city terminology, inserted in the following pages, is intended for a variety of exercises throughout the course. This principle applies to all the illustrations in this book.

Let's describe the picture (or a part of it): Links ist ein altes Rathaus, daneben ist...

links (to the) left	**oben** at the top	**vorn** at the front
rechts (to the) right	**unten** at the bottom	**hinten** at the back
davor in front of (that)	**daneben** next to (that)	**dahinter** behind (that)
in der Mitte in the middle	**im Vordergrund/im Hintergrund** in the fore/background	

EINE DEUTSCHE STADT — A GERMAN CITY

Don't have a nervous breakdown! This is only reference vocabulary for language work with this topic. You pick and choose as appropriate to your task. See p.41 for exercises.

PEOPLE

der Mann(¨er)	man	die Frau(en)	woman	das Kind(er)	child
der Polizist(en)	policeman	der Passant(en)	pedestrian	der Tourist(en)	tourist
die Polizistin(nen)	policewoman	die Passantin(nen)		die Touristin(nen)	
der Herr(n)	(gentle)man	die Dame(n)	lady	das Baby(s)	baby
der Fahrer(-)	driver	der Beifahrer(-)	passenger	der Hund(e)	dog
der Musikant(en)	musician	der Bettler(-)	beggar	derPostbote(n)	postman

BUILDINGS

die Stadt(¨e)	town	das Gebäude(e)	building	*groß	large
das Rathaus(¨er)	town hall	die Kirche(n)	church	*klein	small
das Haus(¨r)	house	der Dom(e)	cathedral	*lang	long
die Burg(en)	castle	das Schloß(¨er)	castle	*kurz	short
das Denkmal(¨er)	monument	der Brunnen(-)	well	*tief	deep
die Schule(n)	school	die Universität(en)	university	*flach	flat
				*hoch	high
				*niedrig	low

FOOD/DRINK

das Café(s)	cafe	das Restaurant(s)	restaurant	*breit	wide
die Kneipe(n)	tavern	das Gasthaus(¨er)	inn, pub	*schmal	narrow
das Hotel(s)	hotel	die Pension(en)	B&B	*neu	new
				*alt	old

ROADS/TRAFFIC

die Straße(n)	road	die Autobahn(en)	motorway	*modern	modern
die Gasse(n)	street	der Platz(¨e)	square	*schön	beautiful
das Trottoir(s)	pavement(Aus.)	der Bürgersteig(e)	pavement	*hübsch	pretty
die Autobahn(en)	motorway	das Autob.kreuz(e)	motorway cross	*viele	many
die Ecke(n)	corner	um die Ecke	round the corner	*weit	far
die Kreuzung(en)	cross roads	die Verkehrsinsel(n)	traffic island	*einige	some
der Übergang(¨e)	crossing	der Zebrastreifen(-)	ped. crossing	*bunt	colourful
die Ampel(n)	traffic lights	der Kreisverkehr(-)	roundabout	*interessant	interesting
der Stau(s)	traffic jam	die Fußgängerzone(n)	ped. precinct	*stark	heavy,strong
der Verkehr(-)	traffic	das Verkehrsamt(¨er)	information office	*leicht	light (traffic)

TRANSPORT

das Auto(s)	car	die Straßenbahn(en)	tram	der Bus(se)	bus
der Zug(¨e)	train	die Bahn(en)	train	der Wagon(e)	carriage
das Taxi(s)	taxi	die Eisenbahn(en)	railway	das Gleis(e)	platform
der Taxistand(¨e)	taxi rank	die Untergrundbahn(en)	underground	der Kiosk(s)	kiosk
die Haltestelle(n)	stop(bus,tram..)	der Bahnhof(¨e)	(railway) station	die Schranke(n)	barrier
der Lastwagen(-)	lorry	der Sattelschlepper(-)	artic. lorry	der Kombi(s)	estate car
das Motorrad(¨er)	motor cycle	der Lieferwagen(¨)	van	das Fahrrad	bycycle
das Flugzeug(e)	aeroplane	der Flughafen(¨)	airport		

POST OFFICE/ BANK

das Postamt(¨er)	post office	der Briefkasten(¨)	post box	die Bank	bank
das Telefon(e)	telephone	der Fernsprecher(-)	public phone	der Bankomat	cash point

PARKING

der Parkplatz(¨e)	car park	das Parkhaus(¨er)	multi storey c.p.	die Parkscheibe(n)	disk
die Strafe(n)	fine	die Parkgebühr(en)	charge	die Parksäule(n)	meter

die Burg(en)
das Stadion
die Kirchen(-)
das Hochhaus(¨er)
PARKHOTEL
RATHAUS
METZGER
GRILL AM MARKT
die Straßenbahn(en)
der Baum(¨er)
das Haus(¨er)
die Haltestelle(n)
der Markt(¨e)
der Bus(se)
der Brunnen(-)
W.C.
LOTTERIE
BUCHHANDLUNG
SCHUHE
KIOSK
das Liebespaar(e)
das Geschäft(¨e)
der Briefkasten(¨)
der Fernsprecher(-)
das Auto(s)
U-Bahnhof
U
der Junge(n)
der Tourist(en)
die Touristin(nen
Ja!
das Baby(s)
die Zeitung(en)
Mmm...
APOTHEKE
die Litfaßsäule(n)
heute
der Hund(e)
der Musikant(en)

der Himmel
die Wolke(n)
das Flugzeug(e)
der Dom(e)
der Flughafen(¨)
der Bahnhof(¨e)
die Uhr(en)
CITIZEN
Uhren
SUPERMARKT
KAUFHAUS
KINO
der Lastwagen(-)
SPEDITION
OPTIK
Alle Richtungen
VOLKS BANK
die Fußgängerzone(n)
POLIZEI
der Lieferwagen(-)
REISEN
das Fahrrad(¨er)
der Radfahrer(-)
ADAC
TAXI
die Kreuzung(en)
der Fahrer(-)
der Pannenhelfer(-)
Zentrum
Parkhaus
Hbf
der Jogger(-)
der Kellner(-)
der Mann(¨er)
das Mädchen(-)
die Frau(en)
das Motorrad(¨er)
das Kind(er)

POLICE

die Polizei	police	die Wachstube(n)	police station	der Streifenwagen	patrol car

HEALTH

das Spital(¨er)	hospital	das Krankenhaus(¨er)	hospital	der Krankenwagen	ambulance
die Klinik(en)	clinic	die Arztpraxis(xen)	surgery	der Optiker	optician

ENTERTAINMENT

das Kino(s)	cinema	das Lokal(e)	establishment	die Disko(s)	disco

SHOPS

das Geschäft(e)	shop	das Kaufhaus(¨er)	department store	der Markt(¨e)	market
das Buchgeschäft	book shop	der Supermarkt(¨e)	supermarket	der Metzger(-)	butcher
die Bäckerei(n)	bakers shop	das Obst/Gemüseg.	fruit/veg. shop	der Friseur(e)	hairdresser
		das Lebensmittelg.	grocer		
die Apotheke(n)	chemist	die Drogerie(n)	drug store		

in der Stadt	in town	auf dem Land	in the country
der Vorort(e)	suburb	am Stadtrand	on the edge of town

* Adjectives suitable for describing the picture

Verbs to help you describe activities:

gehen	to go	fahren	to go, drive	kommen	to come
sitzen	to sit	stehen	to stand	ankommen+	to arrive
liegen	to lie				
einsteigen+ (in)	to get into	aussteigen+(aus)	to get out (of)	abfahren+	to depart
laufen	to run	joggen	to jog	überqueren	to cross
warten	to wait	halten	to stop, to hold	parken	to park
abbiegen+	to turn off	einbiegen+	to turn into	wenden	to turn
essen	to eat	trinken	to drink	bestellen	to order
(be)zahlen	to pay	kaufen	to buy	verkaufen	to sell
				einkaufen+	to shop
hören	to listen	lesen	to read	sprechen	to speak
				unterhalten	to converse
fühlen	to feel	sehen	to see	ansehen+	to look at
besichtigen	to look at sights	schauen	to look	anschauen+	to look at
spielen	to play	lachen	to laugh	weinen	to cry
arbeiten	to work	bauen	to build	reinigen	to clean
fließen	to flow	rinnen	to run (water)	tropfen	to drip
gießen	to water				
geben	to give	tun	to do	stecken	to insert

+ separable verbs (chapter 7)

'to put'

'geben' or **'tun'** in a general context.
'legen' (to lay something on..) for flat objects (e.g. book, paper etc.),
'stellen' (to stand something on..) for tall objects (e.g. bottle, glas etc.)
'stecken' for putting things into confined spaces such as drawers, pockets, letterboxes etc.

links (von)	to the left of	vorn	at the front	davor	in front of (that)
rechts (von)	to the rght of	hinten	at the back	unter	under
unten	at the bottom	neben	next to	ober	above
oben	at the top	hinter	behind	über	over

in der Mitte	in the middle	davor	at the front of that
im Vordergrund	in the foreground	darunter	at the back of that
im Hintergrund	in the background	darüber	over that

Picture based Exercises
(Hints to tutors and students)

Allow the picture to inspire and amuse you.

- **For beginners:** **Vocabulary and present tense practice** i.e. 'Da ist, da sind... Was macht er, sie'?
  'Was tun die Leute'? etc.

  Simple dialogue practice after studying a topic (i.e. shopping for food in the market)

  Cases and prepositions can be practised quite enjoyably by describing all or part of any of the illustrations.

- **For all students:** **Looking at the illustrations only, without any notes,** practise conversations based on the situational dialogues within any of the topic areas, pretend you are shopping, at the post office, at the chemist, at the station, at the airport, in a restaurant, in the tram, in the hotel, on holiday etc. or talking to people in general.

- **Practise tenses:** Pretend any of the actions have already happened (past tenses) or are going to happen (future tense). See pages 193-195.

- **For more advanced students:** Describing the illustrations offers a good opportunity to practise cases, noun and adjectival endings (p.197, once you have learnt cases), and more complicated structures.

If you need to use grammar already learnt but are having trouble with recall, don't rack your brains and waste valuable time, go straight to the Grammar Survey on p.183 and make good use of the information found there.

There are several advantages in doing these picture-related exercises, even at an early stage, as you will automatically absorb useful vocabulary as you scan the picture for suitable nouns.

Boredom, that well-known enemy of effective learning, will perhaps be less of a problem when faced with a bit of humour.

- **Verloren? Gestohlen?** Lost? Stolen?

- **Am Flughafen** At the airport

John: Um Gottes Willen, **meine Aktentasche ist weg!**
He rushes off to report his loss.

Was nun? Meine ganzen Papiere, Dokumente und die Unterlagen für das neue Projekt sind darin!

'die Polizei' police
'das Fundbüro'. lost property office
'Ich möchte eine Verlustanzeige machen' I would like to report losing ...

Official: **Hier ist das Formular!**

John: **Mein Paß, mein Scheckbuch, meine Papiere.... Bitte, hier ist meine Liste!**

Official: **Bitte, unterschreiben Sie hier unten!**

John: *(later)* Das ist zu viel Stress für mich! Ah, hier im Café ist es gemütlich!
(settles down in the corner with a large whisky and starts to read the paper) Die Zeitung ist heute wieder nicht interessant. *(drops off to sleep)*

Waiter: **Haben Sie sonst noch einen Wunsch?**

John: *(wakes up startled)* Was? Wo bin ich? Ach so, nein danke!
(tries to get hold of his briefcase) Wo ist meine Aktentasche? Ach, das ist wie ein schlechter Traum! Vielleicht hat die Polizei oder das Fundbüro gute Nachricht für mich!

- **Im Fundbüro** At the lost property office

John: Haben Sie vielleicht meine Tasche?

Official: **Sie haben Glück,** hier ist sie! Jemand hat sie irrtümlich mitgenommen!

John: **Gott sei Dank! Ich bin sehr froh!**

Official: **Eine kleine Gebühr ist zu bezahlen.** 5 DM, bitte.
Hier ist Ihre Quittung.

verloren	lost	**gestohlen**	stolen
Um Gottes Willen!	Goodness!	**weg**	gone
die Aktentasche(n)	brief-case	**das Dokument(e)**	document
das Papier(e)	paper	**die Unterlagen**	papers,records
das Projekt(e)	project	**das Scheckbuch(¨er)**	cheque-book
das Formular(e)	form	**die Liste(n)**	list
die Gebühr(en)	fee, charge	**die Quittung(en)**	receipt
der Stress	stress	**die Zeitung(en)**	newspaper
der Traum(¨e)	dream	**die Nachricht(en)**	news

Haben Sie sonst noch einen Wunsch?	Is there anything else, you would like?

Sie haben Glück!	You are lucky!	**unterschreiben**	to sign
Gott sei Dank!	Thank God!	**bezahlen**	to pay

schlecht	bad	**ganz**	total, all
froh	happy, glad		
für mich	for me	**darin**	in it
irrtümlich	by mistake		

jemand hat mitgenommen ...	somebody has taken ...

Note: 'Haben Sie vielleicht meine Tasche? Hier ist **sie**'. 'Here **she** is' instead of 'here **it** (es) is'. 'It' refers to 'die Aktentasche', a feminine noun. Therefore 'sie' (she) is used instead of 'es' (it), which only replaces neuter nouns, 'er' (he) is used when 'it' refers to a masculine noun. (Mistakes will hardly be noticed.)

Exercise:

Looking through the previous dialogue and at the list of items (p.44) pretend you need to report the loss of your bag or briefcase. Tell the official what was in your bag by reading out your list (about ten items). You could try to speak freely with only an occasional glance at your notes.

die Tasche(n)	bag	**die Reisetasche**	travelbag
die Ledertasche(n)	leather-bag	**die Mappe(n)**	folder
das Geld(er)	money	**das Kleingeld**	change
der Geldschein(e)	bank-note	**die Münze(n)**	coin
der 10 Mark Schein	ten mark note	**die 5 Mark Münze**	5 mark coin
die Geldbörse(n)	purse	**die Brieftasche(n)**	wallet
das Portemonnaie(s)	purse	**der Geldbeutel(-)**	purse
der Paß(¨sse)	passport	**der Ausweis(e)**	identity card
der Führerschein(e)	driving licence	**die Fahrkarte(n)**	ticket (train etc.)
die Kreditkarte(n)	credit-card	**die Scheckkarte(n)**	cheque-card
die Bankomatkarte(n)	cash-card	**der Reisescheck(s)**	travellers cheques
der Schlüssel(-)	key	**der Schlüsselbund**	bunch of keys
der Photoapparat(e)	camera	**der Film(e)**	film
der Terminkalender(-)	diary	**das Notizbuch(¨er)**	note-book
der Taschenrechner(-)	calculator	**das Mobiltelefon(e)**	mobile phone
die Radioweckuhr(en)	radio alarm-clock	**der Rasierapparat(e)**	shaver
Toilettartikel(-)	toiletries	**der Kamm(¨e)**	comb
der Füller(-)	fountain-pen	**der Kugelschreiber**	(der Kuli)biro
der Bleistift(e)	pencil	**der Filzstift(e)**	felt-pen
die Brille(n)	glasses	**der Schirm(e)**	umbrella
die Sonnenbrille(n)	sun-glasses	**das Taschentuch(¨er)**	handkerchief

Note: In general, additional vocabulary relevant to a chapter can be found in the appendix. For example, the chapter dealing with changing currency at the bank has a considerable extension to its vocabulary found under 'Banking & Finance'; the same applies to the chapters dealing with food and drink, shopping, the world of work etc.

Don't assume for one moment you need to know all these terms, they are only intended as reference material for you or your tutor, to dip into to just browse or to broaden the spectrum of language work undertaken.

CHAPTER 5

Deutschland heute *Germany today*

- Picture and vocabulary. Topic: ' The Countryside '.
- Accusative case and prepositions. Comparative.

Herr Müller: **Viele Leute mit Stadtwohnungen haben ein Wochenendhaus** im Grünen.
Manche kaufen einen Baugrund und bauen ein Haus oder einen Bungalow.

John: Der Lebensstandard in Deutschland, Österreich und der Schweiz scheint recht gut zu sein.

Herr Müller: Das stimmt im Großen und Ganzen. Wir arbeiten nicht nur, wir leben auch gern gut.

Es gibt seit der Wiedervereinigung gewaltige wirtschaftliche Probleme in beiden Teilen Deutschlands.

John: Aber man sieht überall Wohlstand. Städte und Dörfer sehen sehr gepflegt aus. Wo sind die Krisengebiete? **Im Osten oder auch im Westen?**

Herr Müller: Fast überall, auch **im Norden und Süden**. Millionen Arbeitslose, Inländer und Ausländer. Integrationsprobleme, Armut u.s.w.

Exercise:	Leben alle Deutsche in Wohnungen? Arbeiten sie nur viel? Wie ist der Lebensstandard in Deutschland etc.? Wie heißt 'reunification' auf Deutsch? Wo gibt es Probleme? Was für Probleme gibt es?

John: *(looking at some photos of Bavaria)* Das ist doch der Königsee! Und der Berg dahinter heißt Watzmann, nicht wahr?

Herr Müller: Richtig, hier ist unser Ferienhaus, ein typisches Bauernhaus.
Das Gebiet ist sehr schön. Viel Landwirtschaft, keine Industrie, keine Umweltprobleme.

John:	Die Landschaft ist einfach wunderbar! Berge, Seen, Felder, Wälder und hübsche Städte und Dörfer.
Herr Müller:	Meine Eltern wohnen noch hier, aber sie kommen oft zu uns nach Frankfurt. **Sie lassen das Auto daheim und nehmen den Zug**, das ist besser für meinen Vater. Weniger Stress.
John:	**Wie ist das Wetter** im Winter in Bayern? Kalt und viel Schnee?
Herr Müller:	Ja, dann ist Hochsaison für Wintersport in den Alpen. **Schifahren ist ein sehr beliebter Sport** und Tausende fahren jährlich auf Schiurlaub. **Im Sommer geht man wandern, Wassersport ist auch sehr populär.**

Exercise:	Hat Bayern viele Umweltprobleme? Warum ist das Gebiet schön? Wie fahren die Eltern von Herrn Müller nach Frankfurt? Was machen viele Leute im Sommer? Und im Winter?

Refer to the vocabulary section for appropriate additional terms for both exercises.

das Wochenendhaus(¨er)	weekend house	**im Grünen**	in the country
der Baugrund(¨e)	building plot	**der Bungalow(s)**	bungalow
der Lebensstandard	living-standard	**der Wohlstand**	prosperity
die Wiedervereinigung	reunification	**das Dorf(¨er)**	village
das Gebiet(e)	area	**die Krise(n)**	crisis
im Westen	in the west	**im Osten**	in the east
im Süden	in the south	**im Norden**	in the north
der/die Arbeitslose	unemployed person	**die Armut**	poverty
der Inländer(-)	national of a country	**der Ausländer(-)**	foreign national, foreigner
der Berg(e)	mountain	**der See(n)**	lake
das Feld(er)	field	**die Landschaft(en)**	landscape
das Ferienhaus(¨er)	holiday-home	**das Bauernhaus(¨er)**	farm-house
die Ferien	vacations	**der Urlaub(e)**	holiday

die Landwirtschaft	agriculture	**die Industrie(n)**	industry
die Alpen	the Alps	**die Umwelt**	environment
die Eltern	parents	**der Stress**	stress
der Zug(¨e)	train	**das Wetter**	weather
der Winter	winter	**der Schnee**	snow
der Sport	sport	**der Wintersport**	winter-sports
der Schiurlaub(e)	skiing holiday	**die Hochsaison**	high-season
der Sommer	summer	**der Wassersport**	water-sports
kaufen	to buy	**bauen**	to build
leben	to live		
fahren	to go, drive	**lassen**	to let
nehmen	to take	**sehen**	to see

Check vowel changes in the 'du' and 'he', 'she', it' forms of the present tense of **'fahren'**, **'lassen'**, **'sehen'** and **'nehmen'** in the list of irregular verbs, p.200-202, second column. The plural forms remain unchanged.
Look back into chapter 2, 'sprechen'.

Exercise: Write out the complete present tense forms of the four irregular verbs above.

aussehen(s.)*	to look like	* Separable verbs: See chapter 7.	
schifahren(s.)*	to ski		
scheinen	to seem	**sein**	to be (chapter 2)
zu uns	to us		
beliebt	popular	**daheim**	at home
gepflegt	well looked after	**überall**	everywhere
kalt	cold	**gewaltig**	enormous
typisch	typical	**besonders**	particularly
weniger	less	**wunderbar**	wonderful

den a form of the definite article 'der' (see next page)
im Großen und Ganzen on the whole

The articles	'der' 'die' 'das' 'ein' 'eine' 'ein'	(chapter 1) are used for the so-called **Nominative Case.**	

The change below is known as the **Accusative Case. It only affects the masculine article 'der', 'ein'** (See Grammar Survey p.197: Table of Cases, also showing the endings on adjectives.)

Accusative Case

'der' ⇒ **'den'** changes to 'ein' ⇒ **'einen'**	**for the direct object in a sentence:** Der Mann sieht **den** Park (einen Park) subject verb object		
after the following prepositions:	**durch** (through) **ohne** (without) **für** (for) **um** (around) **gegen** (against) **entlang** (along) Der Mann geht **durch den** (ein**en**) Park		

and when movement (→) is implied: (See also: Chapter 8)	**in** (in) **auf** (on) **an** (at) **neben** (next to) **vor**(in front of) **hinter** (at the back of) **unter**(under) **ober** (above) **über** (above) **zwischen** (between) Der Mann geht **in den** (ein**en**) Garten (The man goes → into the (a) garden)

Don't worry! In all foreign languages there is a certain amount of underlying grammar which needs to be referred to occasionally. As I have said in the introduction, if you are just aiming at survival proficiency you need to concentrate on core knowledge only and grammar need not bother you too much.
As we go along, there will be more grammar points to be considered, take note and don't allow yourself to be put off! Don't expect to be able to use everything you are taught absolutely perfectly straightaway. Eventually, however, everything will fall into place and you will be surprised how logical it all is.

In practice, case mistakes won't affect the meaning of what you are saying, when you are trying to speak. Only if you want to go on to more advanced studies will you have to be able to apply grammar more consistently. The Grammar Survey at the end of this book will provide you with a comprehensive but easily understood, compact summary of all the grammatical points made in the text. For now, look at the table of cases (p.197) and just note in the first instance that certain endings are found in conjunction with each case. Regard them with interest (after all, English had similar endings originally) and keep your finger between the pages because for the next exercise you will have to refer to them.

Nominative/Accusative?	Ein warm-- Mantel für d-- Winter.(der Mantel - coat) Ein- rot- Bluse für d-- Sommer.(die Bluse - blouse) Viele Deutsche haben ein-- gut-- Lebensstandard. Sie sehen hier ein-- klein-- See. Wir nehmen d-- Intercity Zug. Ich komme ohne mein-- Wagen.(der Wagen - car) Wo parken Sie d-- groß- Auto? Das Boot fährt um d-- schön-- See.

Was sehen Sie auf dem Bild: 'Eine deutsche Landschaft'?

Ich sehe/wir sehen:	**den**/**einen** hohen Berg (m.) die/eine alte Burg (f.) das/ein neues Haus (n.)

The Comparative:

In English we say:	big - bigg**er** but	beautiful - **more** beautiful
In German:	only the **-er** ending is used	
	nett nett**er** klein klein**er**	
	often there is a vowel change	
	groß grö**ßer** lang läng**er**	

'than'	as in longer than..... is translated by: 'als'
'als'	**länger als.....**

Write down five comparisons using one of the pictures as your inspiration.

groß	**größer**	klein	klein**er**	kurz	**kürzer**	lang	**länger**
hoch	**höher**	tief	tief**er**	breit	breit**er**	alt	**älter**
schön	schön**er**	kalt	**kälter**	heiß	heiß**er**	warm	**wärmer**

der Himmel
der Gletscher(-)
der Schnee
das Eis
der Drachenflieger(-)
der Hubschrauber(-)
die Wolke(n)
der Berg(e)
die Stadt(¨e)
der Hügel(-)
die Fabrik(en)
der Sessellift(e)
der Schilift(e)
der Zug(¨e)
der Tunnel(-)
die Brücke(n)
die Tankstelle(n)
der See(n)
das Segelboot(e)
das Schiff(e)
das Dorf(¨er)
das Schloß(¨er)
der Bus(se)
der Stau(s)
der Sportplatz(¨e)
die Insel(n)
das Ufer(-)
die Baustelle(n)
die Autobahn(en)
der Spielplatz(¨e)
der Campingplatz(¨e)
das Zelt(e)
das Feld(er)
der Krankenwagen(-)
der Bauernhof(¨e)
der Wasserfall(¨e)
der Polizist(en)
das Pferd(e)
der Unfall(¨e)
der Fluß(¨sse)
die Wiese(n)
der Weg(e)
der Fels(en)
die Seilbahn(en)
das Wasser
der Sonnenschirm(e)
der Baum(¨e)
der Wegweiser(-)
der Wald(¨er)
die Kuh(¨e)
die Familie(n)
das Gras
der Pilz(e)
der Hase(n)
der Stein(e)
die Schnecke(n)
der Vogel(¨)
die Blume(n)
die Ameise(n)

EINE DEUTSCHE LANDSCHAFT Vocabulary Topic: A GERMAN LANDSCAPE

This vocabulary is for reference and will help you with language tasks related to this topic.
Did you think you had to learn it all?

LANDSCAPE FEATURES

der Berg(e)	mountain
der Gipfel(-)	summit
das Gebirge(-)	moutain range
der Hügel(-)	hill
der Fels(en)	rock
der Stein(e)	stone
das Tal(¨er)	valley
die Schlucht(en)	gorge
der Fluß(¨sse)	river
das Ufer(-)	bank
der Bach(¨e)	stream
der See(n)	lake
der Kanal(¨e)	canal
das Boot(e)	boat
das Segelboot(e)	sailing boat
das Ruderboot(e)	rowing boot
das Schiff (e)	ship
der Dampfer(-)	pleasure boat
das Paddelboot	canoe
der Gletscher(-)	glacier
der Schnee(-)	snow
das Eis	ice
das Wasser	water
der Wasserfall(¨e)	waterfall

LANDSCAPE FEATURES

der Wald(¨er)	wood
der Hang(¨e)	slope
die Wiese(n)	meadow
das Feld(er)	field
der Acker(¨er)	field
der Weg(e)	path
der Rain(e)	verge
der Rucksack(¨e)	rucksack
die Karte(n)	map

TRANSPORT

die Straße(n)	road
die Autobahn(en)	motorway
die Bundesstraße(n)	A-road
die Tankstelle(n)	petrol station
die Seilbahn(en)	cable-car
der Sessellift(e)	chair lift
der Schilift(e)	ski lift
der Hubschrauber	helicopter
der Campingplatz	camp site
das Zelt(e)	tent
der Spielplatz(¨e)	play ground
der Sportplatz(¨e)	sports ground

ANIMALS

der Hund(e)	dog
die Katze(n)	cat
das Pferd(e)	horse
die Kuh(¨e)	cow
das Reh(e)	deer
der Hirsch(e)	stag
der Hase(n)	hare
das Kaninchen(-)	rabbit
der Vogel(¨)	bird
der Schmetterling(e)	butterfly
der Falter(-)	butterfly
die Biene(n	bee
der Zug(¨e)	train
die Eisenbahn(en)	train
die Brücke(n)	bridge
der Tunnel(-)	tunnel
das Hotel(s)	hotel
die Hütte(n)	hut
die Raststätte(n)	motel
die Pension(en)	pension, B&B
der Himmel	sky
die Wolke(en)	cloud
der Wind(e)	wind
der Regen	rain

das Krankenhaus(¨er)	hospital
der Krankenwagen	ambulance
einen Unfall haben	to have an accident (chapter 16)

PEOPLE

der Mann(¨er)	man
der Polizist(en)	policeman
die Polizistin(nen)	policewoman
der Herr(n)	(gentle)man
der Fahrer(-)	driver
der Tourist(en)	tourist
die Touristin(nen)	
die Frau(en)	woman
der Passant(en)	pedestrian
die Passantin(nen)	ditto, f.
die Dame(n)	lady
der Beifahrer(-)	passenger
der Wanderer(-)	walker
die Wanderin(nen)	ditto, f.
das Kind(er)	child
das Baby(s)	baby
der Kletterer	climber
die Kletterin	ditto, f.

BUILDINGS

die Stadt(¨e)	town
das Dorf(¨er)	village
das Haus(¨er)	house
das Gebäude(e)	building
die Kirche(en)	church
das Bauernhaus(¨er)	farmhouse
der Bauernhof(¨e)	ditto
die Burg(en)	castle
das Schloß(¨sser)	castle
die Fabrik(en)	factory

Further vocabulary to help you describe activities:

gehen	to go	fahren	to go, drive	kommen	to come
sitzen	to sit	stehen	to stand	ankommen+	to arrive
liegen	to lie				
einsteigen+ (in)	to get into	aussteigen+(aus)	to get out (of)	abfahren+	to depart
laufen	to run	joggen	to jog	überqueren	to cross
warten	to wait	halten	to stop, to hold	parken	to park
abbiegen+	to turn off	einbiegen+	to turn into	wenden	to turn
essen	to eat	trinken	to drink	bestellen	to order
(be)zahlen	to pay	kaufen	to buy	verkaufen	to sell
				einkaufen+	to shop
hören	to listen	lesen	to read	sprechen	to speak
				unterhalten	to converse
fühlen	to feel	sehen	to see	ansehen+	to look at
besichtigen	to look at sights	schauen	to look	anschauen+	to look at
spielen	to play	lachen	to laugh	weinen	to cry
arbeiten	to work	bauen	to build	reinigen	to clean
fließen	to flow	rinnen	to run (water)	tropfen	to drip
gießen	to water				
geben	to give	tun	to do	stecken	to insert

einen Picknick machen	to have a picnic	einen Ausflug machen	to go on an outing
eine Wanderung machen	to go on a hike	die Aussicht bewundern	to admire the view

\+ separable verbs (chapter 7)

> **'to put'** is expressed in a general context by using **'geben'** or **'tun'**. More specifically **'legen'** (to lay something on..) for flat objects (e.g. book, paper etc.), **'stellen'** (to stand something on..) for tall objects (e.g. bottle, glas etc.) while **'stecken'** is used for putting things into confined spaces such as drawers, letter-boxes...

*groß	large	*einige	some	*weit	far	Colours: see appendix
*klein	small	*bunt	colourful	*hügelig	hilly	
*lang	long	*tief	deep	*flach	flat	
*kurz	short	*viele	many	*gebirgig	mountainous	
*hoch	high	*hübsch	pretty	*stark	strong, heavy (e.g. rain)	
*breit	wide	*schön	beautiful	*interessant	interesting	

*schmal	narrow	links (von)	to the left of	vorn	at the front	davor	in front of..
*alt	old	rechts (von)	to the right of	hinten	at the back	unter	under
*neu	new	unten	at the bottom	neben	next to	ober	above
*modern	modern	oben	at the top	hinter	behind	über	over

in der Mitte	in the middle	davor	at the front of that
im Vordergrund	in the foreground	darunter	at the back of that
im Hintergrund	in the background	darüber	over that

- **For beginners:** Vocabulary practice, 'Da ist, da sind... Present tense, 'Was macht er, sie? Was tun die Leute?'
- **For all students:** After completing the relevant chapters you can allow the picture to inspire and amuse you and go in for some additional practice: Imagine you are at the railway station, at the airport, in an alpine restaurant using terms you have learnt. Or you could buy tickets for a bus ride or trip in a cable-car etc. You can also tell people where you come from, where you are going, how you like your holiday...
- **Practise tenses** by pretending any of the actions have already happened (past tenses) or are going to happen (future tense).
- **Oral practice:** What are people saying to one another?
- **For more advanced students *:** A good oppurtunity to practise cases, nouns and adj. endings, p197.

- **Am Bahnhof** At the station

John:	**Bitte, wann fährt der nächste Zug nach München?**
Official:	Der Intercity (IC) fährt in 20 Minuten, um halb fünf.
John:	Wie bitte, um 17 Uhr 30?
Official:	Nein, **um halb fünf, das ist 16 Uhr 30.**
John:	Ja, natürlich, Sie haben recht. **Eine Rückfahrkarte, bitte.**
Official:	Also, **eine Karte, hin und zurück, erste oder zweite Klasse?**
John:	**Zweite Klasse, bitte.**
Official:	125 DM und **50 DM Zuschlag,** das macht 175 DM.
John:	100 DM, 50 DM und zwei Zehner und 5 Mark, stimmt's?
Official:	Ja, **Ihre Karte, Bahnsteig 5**.
John:	Danke, **fährt der Zug direkt oder muß ich umsteigen?.**
Official:	Dieser Zug fährt direkt.
John:	**Welcher Anschluß ist** dann für Berchtesgaden **am besten?**
Official:	Einen Moment, bitte, ich muß im Fahrplan nachsehen. Also, Sie haben zehn Minuten nach Ihrer Ankunft Anschluß.

(Telling the time, p.147)

der Bahnhof(¨e)	railway station	**die Karte(n)**	ticket
der Zug(¨e)	train	**die einfache Karte**	single ticket
der Bahnsteig(e)	platform	**die Rückfahrkarte**	return ticket
(das Gleis)		**für Erwachsene**	for adults
der Anschluß(¨sse)	connection	**für Kinder**	for children
die Ankunft	arrival	**der Platz(¨e)**	seat, berth
die Abfahrt	departure	**reservieren**	to reserve
um halb fünf	at half past **four**	**der Fahrplan(¨e)**	time-table
		nachsehen	to check
der nächste Zug	the next train		
Fährt der Zug direkt?	Is it a direct train?	**hin und zurück**	there and back
Muß ich umsteigen?	Do I have to change?	**der Zuschlag(¨e)**	surcharge

dieser, diese, dieses	this	**welcher, welcher, welches**	which

(They follow the same pattern re. endings as the definite article, p197.)

Sie haben recht!	You are right!	**Stimmt's?**	Correct?
Die Auskunft(¨e)	information	**die Reise(n)**	journey
der Schalter(-)	counter	**fahren**	to travel
		reisen	to travel
die Fahrkarte(n)	ticket (trains, buses etc.)	**der Automat(en)**	machine
der Fahrkartenautomat	ticket dispenser		

Scan the terminology in the previous dialogue, the vocabulary following and the phrases below. Having acquired almost complete 'railway' competence it should not be difficult to complete the following exercise.

Exercise:

Ask for a single 1st class ticket to Köln.
Ask for a return ticket, 2nd class, to Munich for two adults and three children.
You would like to reserve a seat.
You would like to reseve five berths in a sleeping car.
What is the cost of these tickets?
You would like a time-table.
At what time does the train arrive in Munich?

	Sitzplatz (erster, zweiter Klasse)		**der Speisewagen**	dining car
einen	**Liegewagenplatz**	**reservieren**	**der Liegewagen**	couchette
	Schlafwagenplatz		**der Schlafwagen**	sleeper

Was kostet eine Karte nach ...?	How much is a ticket to ...?
Muß ich Zuschlag zahlen?	Do I have to pay a surcharge?
Hat der Zug einen Speisewagen?	Is there a dining car on the train?
Wann kommt der Zug nach ...	When does the train arrive in...?
Haben Sie noch Plätze?	Have you still got any seats?
Ich möchte ...	I would like ...

- **Der falsche Zug** The wrong train

John goes to platform four, having mistaken 'fünf' for 'vier' (a common mistake). While admiring the rather sleek Intercity (IC) opposite, a rather more basic looking 'Nahverkehrszug' (local stopping train) pulls in. He gets in and sits down in a very crowded compartment.

John: **Entschuldigen Sie, ist das der Intercity nach München?**

Passenger: (laughing) Nein, hier sind wir nicht im Intercity. Dort ist es viel luxuriöser.
Der Intercity fährt von Bahnsteig 5 ab.

John: Um Gottes Willen! Der fährt ja gleich, **das ist mein Zug!**
Hoffentlich versäume ich meine Sitzung nicht.
(rushes off at high speed)

Um Gottes Willen!	Good God!	**abfahren**	to depart
die Sitzung(en)	meeting	**versäumen**	to miss
luxuriös	luxurious	**gleich**	straight away

It is worth noting that the railway-system in Germany, Austria and Switzerland is very efficient and well worth using. There are excellent and frequent Intercity services as well as very comfortable trans-continental long distance train connections travelling through some of the most beautiful countryside in Europe.

Train fares are very reasonable since they are still state-subsidised. Information is readily available from the Tourist Offices of the respective countries or their offices abroad.

Practise telling the time (p.147), particularly 'half past...' as mistakes are often made here and result in embarassing, totally avoidable misunderstandings.

CHAPTER 6

Wien, eine wunderbare Stadt. *Vienna, a wonderful city*

- Conversation about towns and Vienna, the capital of Austria.
- Superlative, dative case and prepositions, 'können', 'müssen' and word-order.
- Eine Fahrt mit dem Taxi. (A taxi drive.)

John: *(looking at more photos)* **Ich sehe hier wunderschöne Landschaftsgebiete, wie sind denn die Städte? Ich kenne nur Frankfurt.**

Herr Müller: **Seit dem Krieg teils neu und modern. Aber es gibt auch viele sehr alte, geschichtlich interessante Städte.**

John: **Frankfurt ist ja hypermodern. Neue Geschäfte, moderne Kaufhäuser, ultramoderne Bankgebäude, Büros und Hochhäuser.**

Exercise:	Wie sind deutsche Landschaften? Sind alle deutschen Städte modern? Seit wann sind sie neu und modern? Hat Frankfurt viele alte Geschäfte? Was gibt es noch in Frankfurt?

Herr Müller: **Ich bin oft geschäftlich in anderen Städten wie Hamburg oder München, aber am liebsten bin ich in Wien, der Hauptstadt Österreichs.**

John: Leider kenne ich Wien nicht, das ist sicher eine Stadt mit angenehmer Atmosphäre.

Herr Müller: Das Leben ist dort nicht so hektisch, irgendwie gemütlicher. Auch finde ich die Bauten aus der Zeit der Habsburger Monarchie faszinierend.

Man kann auch die meisten Sehenswürdigkeiten zu Fuß besichtigen.
Sie sind fast alle im Stadtzentrum und dort ist überall Fußgängerzone.

John: Aber Wien ist groß, wie kommt man da in andere Bezirke?

Herr Müller:	**Man kann mit der Straßenbahn, mit der U-Bahn oder mit dem Bus fahren.** **Die öffentlichen Verkehrsmittel sind ausgezeichnet.**
John:	Und die vielen Cafés und Restaurants sowie die berühmten Caféhäuser und Heurigen! Die Stadt ist sehr romantisch, denke ich.
Herr Müller:	Sie sind ja schon gut informiert, da müssen Sie Wien wirklich bald kennenlernen.

Exercise:	Macht Herr Müller oft Urlaub in Hamburg? Wohin fahren Sie manchmal? Geschäftlich oder auf Urlaub? Sind die Verkehrsmittel hier ausgezeichnet? Nennen Sie fünf Verkehrsmittel. (Picture: 'Eine deutsche Stadt') In welcher Stadt sind Sie am liebsten? Warum?

der Krieg(e)	war	**Wie?**	How, what ..like?
		wie	as, like
das Kaufhaus(¨er)	store	**seit**	since
das Hochhaus(¨er)	sky-scraper	**wunderschön**	marvellous
die Bank(en)	bank	**teils**	partly, in part
		neu	new
das Gebäude(-)	building		
der Bau(ten)	building	**geschichtlich**	historic
		geschäftlich	on business
die Hauptstadt(¨e)	capital	**ander-**(+ending)	other
die Atmosphäre(n)	atmosphere		
das Leben	life	**am liebsten**	best of all
		angenehm	pleasant
die Sehenswürdigkeit(en)	sights		
der Bezirk(e)	district	**hektisch**	hectic
die Straßenbahn(en)	tram	**gemütlich**	relaxing
öffentliche Verkehrsmittel	public transport	**die meisten**	most

der Heurige(n)	Wine-bar where delicious food is also always available. Found in the vineyards round Vienna, well worth visiting because of their friendly, welcoming atmosphere. The Viennese seem to spend all their evenings there!

die Habsburger Monarchie	the Hapsburg Monarchy: Empire in Central Europe of some 54 million people (1914) which lasted about a 1000 years until 1918. Its capital city was Vienna.

faszinierend	fascinating	**wirklich**	really
berühmt	famous	**bald**	soon
besichtigen	to look at, view	**kennenlernen**	to get to know
informieren	to inform	**denken**	to think

können	to be able, can	**müssen**	to have to, must
ich kann (I can)	**wir können**	**ich muß** (I must)	**wir müssen**
du kannst	**ihr könnt**	**du mußt**	**ihr müsst**
Sie können	**Sie können**	**Sie müssen**	**Sie müssen**
er		**er**	
sie kann	**sie können**	**sie muß**	**sie müssen**
es		**es**	

Ich kann morgen nicht **kommen.**
Können Sie den Zug **sehen?**

Ich muß jetzt **telefonieren.**
Wir müssen nach Bonn **fahren.**

Note the position of the second verb at the end of the sentence.

Ich muß nicht	I don't have to	**never**	I must not (see 'dürfen', p.73)

Translate:	You must come now!	(All forms of 'you')
	Can you see the house?	(All forms of 'you')
	Do we have to take the car?	
	Does he have to go now?	
	Can she ski?	

	Comparative	**Superlative**
schön (beautiful)	schön**er** (more beautiful)	**am** schön**sten** (most beautiful)
klein (small)	klein**er** (smaller)	**am** klein**sten** (smallest)
gut (good)	bess**er** (better)	**am** bes**ten** (best of all)
hoch (high)	höh**er** (higher)	**am** höch**sten** (highest)

There is no 'more' and 'most' in German comparisons, as in 'more' and 'most beautiful' just 'schön**er**' and 'am schön**sten**'.

Comparatives and Superlatives can be used as adjectives: 'der kleinere Apfel', 'der kleinste Apfel' but 'der Apfel ist am kleinsten'.

Exercises:

Choose five items from one of the pictures and make comparisons. There is a useful list of adjectives with each picture, ask your tutor for help (or use a dictionary) if you are not sure about an 'Umlaut' on the comparative or superlative.

Example: (Look at the illustration, p.38)
Das Kind links ist **kleiner als** die Frau rechts.
Das Baby links ist **größer als** der Teddy.
Aber der Vogel auf der Straße ist **am kleinsten.**

How to express liking and preferences by adding the following terms to the verb:

gern	**lieber**	**am liebsten**
Ich esse **gern**...	Ich esse **lieber**...	Ich esse **am liebsten**...
I like eating...	**I prefer** eating...	**I like best of all** to eat...

Look at 'Food and Drink' (p.152-157) and write down what you like, prefer and like best to eat and drink.

- **Im Taxi zum Flughafen** To the airport by taxi

- A conversation with a foreign taxi-driver

John: *(in Herrn Müllers office)* **Ich muß für nachmittag ein Taxi bestellen.**
Mein Flug ist um 5 Uhr.

Herr Müller: Einen Moment, ich habe die Nummer hier. **Taxiruf: 870-31-315. Dieser Taxistand ist ganz in der Nähe, von dort kommen die Taxis am schnellsten.**

John: *(dials)* **Hallo! Bitte, ich möchte ein Taxi für viertel nach drei bestellen.**

Voice: Also fünfzehn Uhr fünfzehn. **Ihre Adresse bitte?**

John: Kornfeldstraße 3.

John: **Zum Flughafen, bitte. Wie lange fahren wir da?**

Driver: Ungefähr eine halbe Stunde, oft aber länger.
Der Verkehr ist heute wieder schrecklich!

John: Gott sei Dank habe ich diesmal genug Zeit! Sind Sie aus Frankfurt?

Driver: Nein, ich bin Ausländer. Ich komme aus Spanien.

John: Sie sprechen prima Deutsch, finde ich.

Driver: Meine Kinder sprechen noch besser. Sie gehen hier in die Schule.
Sie kommen aus England, nicht wahr?

John: Richtig, kennen Sie England?

Driver: Ja, ich war schon oft in London, sehr interessant!

John: Ah, hier ist schon der Flughafen, das war aber schnell.
Was macht das, bitte?

Driver: 45 DM, bitte.

John: **Hier sind 50 DM, das stimmt so.**

Driver: **Vielen Dank und gute Reise!**

When rounding up a bill or giving a tip **(Trinkgeld)** the approprate phrases are:

'das stimmt so' or **'das ist für Sie'**

Tips: In German speaking countries, as indeed in most other Continental countries, tips are customary and given without any feelings of embarrasssment. The basic wages in the service industries are not high, therefore tipping is expected and has always been a way of life. 5% to 10% are about right as restaurant bills normally show a service charge.

'Ausländer' (foreigners) are quite an emotive issue. Large numbers of people from countries round the Mediterranean were originally invited to come and work in German firms because of a shortage of labour in the fifties.
Many of these original immigrants known as **'Gastarbeiter'** have become naturalised. They and their children have largely become integrated and all was well while the German economy was bouyant.

As a result of the recession of recent years, the added cost of the reunification (the former DDR needed and still needs colossal amounts of money investing in it), mounting unemployment, the ever increasing numbers of refugees from Eastern Europe and the rest of the world, as well as even larger numbers of illegal immigrants being smuggled in by organised gangs in return for considerable sums, Germany's economic stability has suffered considerably and the financial strains are beginning to be felt.

This has caused a certain amount of unease and worry among the population and has been used as a pretext for unacceptable behaviour by criminally inclined individuals claiming allegiance to illegal right-wing political groups. The majority of Germans, Austrians and Swiss people though are a thoroughly decent and good-natured lot.

We have learnt about the **Nominative** (p.48), the basic form of the article and the **Accusative**, where the article changes from der ⇒ **den** (p. 48). As we have seen, articles are also affected if they follow certain words, called prepositions.
After a number of these words (see p.62) the article changes to what is known as the Dative Case.

Dative Case

sg.

(m.)			(f.)			(n.)		
der	⇒	**dem**	die	⇒	**der**	das	⇒	**dem**
ein	⇒	ein**em**	eine	⇒	ein**er**	ein	⇒	ein**em**

pl.

die	⇒	**den**
kein	⇒	kein**en**

Dative prepositions:

(see p.61, also Grammar Survey in the appendix, p.197)

mit (with) **zu** (to) **aus** (out of, from) **bei** (nearby, at) **nach** (after, past) **von** (from) **seit** (since) **gegenüber** (opposite).

When **no movement** is implied some more prepositions take the dative case e.g. **in** (in) **auf** (on) **an** (at) **neben** (next to) **vor** (in front of) **hinter** (at the back of) **unter** (under) **ober** (above) **über** (above) and **zwischen** (between) .

All endings on adjectives are '-en' mit **dem** rot**en** Bus in **der** lang**en** Straße

Some examples

(m.)	der Bus		**mit**	**dem**	Bus
(f.)	die Straßenbahn	but	**in**	**der**	Straßenbahn
(n)	das Taxi		**aus**	**dem**	Taxi

Abbreviations

in dem	⇒	**im**	an/auf dem	⇒	**am**
zu dem	⇒	**zum**	bei dem	⇒	**beim**
zu der	⇒	**zur**	von dem	⇒	**vom**

Dative Practice

Use the correct form of the article in the exercise below:
Ich bin in d-- Bus. Das Taxi fährt auf d-- Straße. Der Garten ist neben d-- Haus. Wir essen in ein-- Restaurant. Man trinkt von ein-- Glas. Bei d-- Haus ist ein Baum.

Now look at the abbreviations and substitute them in the exercise above where appropriate.

Make corrections to the articles in the following exercise using the information about the Dative Case: e.g. 'mit der Bus' corrected to 'mit **dem** Bus':
in der Zug, in die Hauptstadt, in das Haus, zu der Garten, zu die Frau, zu das Kind, aus der Flughafen, bei die U- Bahn, neben das Büro, von der Berg, unter die Alpen.

Using the prepositions above and the information on the pictures to describe all or part of one of the pictures, e.g. Life in a German Town or any of the other illustrations.
Da ist ein Markt vor dem Rathaus, auf der Straße ist ein Auto neben einem Bus etc. (Add adjectives if you like, remembering that all their endings are '-en' in the Dative.)

CHAPTER 7

Ein Wochenende in Wien *A weekend in Vienna*

- Using the phone to book hotel accommodation in Vienna.
- Separable verbs, 'sollen', 'wollen', 'möchten' and their effect on word order.
- Making a start on pronouns and their cases.

John: **Ich muß sagen, ich möchte Wien bald kennenlernen.**

Herr Müller: **Gute Idee! Warum machen wir nicht gemeinsam einen Kurzurlaub in Wien? Dieses Wochenende!**

Am Freitag ist hier in Deutschland ein Feiertag und ich kann den Montag freinehmen. Was meinen Sie?

John: **Wunderbar! Ich bin einverstanden. Wann müssen wir wegfahren** und um wieviel Uhr soll ich startbereit sein?

Herr Müller: Gleich nach dem Frühstück. **Um neun Uhr, denke ich. Die Fahrt dauert fast einen ganzen Tag** und wir wollen auch unterwegs Pausen machen. Manchmal gibt es auch starken Verkehr.

John: Das finde ich eine prima Idee. **Ich muß schnell David anrufen.** Er ist gerade bei seiner Freundin hier in Frankfurt.

(on the phone) **Hallo, Britta, hier spricht John. Kann ich bitte David sprechen?**

Britta: Selbstverständlich, ich rufe ihn gleich. Daaaaaaaaaaaaavid!

David: **Hallo, John! Was ist los?**

John: Herr Müller und ich haben einen ausgezeichneten Plan. **Wir wollen dieses Wochenende nach Wien fahren. Kommt Ihr auch?**

David: **Das geht leider nicht.** Brittas Bruder kommt uns besuchen.

John: Schade, wir fahren mit dem Wagen, Herrn Müllers Mercedes. Das ist ein super Auto, sicher und bequem.

John: **Wir fahren am Freitag hin und kommen am Montag zurück. Kannst Du mich am Montag bei der geplanten Besprechung vertreten?**

David: **Kein Problem, das geht ohne weiteres.**

die Idee(n)	idea	**kennenlernen(s.)***	to get to know
der Kurzurlaub(e)	short holiday	**freinehmen(s.)**	to take time off
		wegfahren(s.)	to leave (a place)
das Wochenende(n)	weekend	**anrufen(s.)**	to call (phone)
der Montag(e)	Monday	**rufen**	to call (somebody)
der Freitag(e)	Friday	**besuchen**	to visit
		denken	to think
der Feiertag	national holiday		
der Feierabend	the time after you stop work	**sollen**	should, ought to
		wollen	to want
die Fahrt(en)	drive, journey		
der Wagen(-)	car	**dauern**	to take (time)
die Pause(n)	break	**vertreten**	to stand in for...

die Besprechung(en)	meeting (informal discussion among just a few people)		
die Sitzung(en)	business meeting (more formal than above)		
Urlaub machen	to go on holiday	**Um wieviel Uhr?**	At what time?
eine Pause machen	to have a break	**startbereit sein**	to be ready to go
das geht (nicht)	that is (not) possible	**ohne weiteres**	no problem
einverstanden	fine, agreed	**Kein Problem!**	No problem!
gemeinsam	jointly	**gleich**	immediately
unterwegs	en route	**stark**	heavy, strong
		ausgezeichnet	excellent
gerade	just now	**schade**	it is a pity
sicher	safe	**bequem**	comfortable
ohne	without		
ausgezeichnet	excellent	**geplant**	planned

Du	you (fam. sg.)	**Ihr**	you (fam. pl.)

(Capitals on 'Du' and 'Ihr': when used as a form of address)

some personal pronouns + accusative forms

ich (I) — **mich** (me)

er (he) — **ihn** (him)

* **(s.) separable verb** (next page)

Separable Verbs marked **(s.)**

Many German verbs have separable prefixes i.e. **'weg'-** on **wegfahren**.
In the infinitive prefix and verb are one word but in a statement or question the prefix goes to the end of the sentence (see below).

Infinitive	statement	question
wegfahren (to go away)	Wir **fahren** morgen abend **weg.**	Wann **fahren** wir **weg?**
anrufen (to phone)	Ich **rufe** in zehn Minuten **an**.	**Rufen** Sie mich **an**?

In combination with modal verbs (können, möchten, müssen, sollen, wollen) prefix and verb stay together:

Wir **können** am Freitag **wegfahren**. Ich **muß** morgen **anrufen**.

We have already met the modal verbs 'können' and 'müssen', we will now learn

'sollen', 'wollen' and 'möchten'

sollen	should, ought to	**wollen**	to want (to)
ich soll (I should)	**wir sollen**	**ich will** (I want)	**wir wollen**
du sollst	**ihr sollt**	**du willst**	**ihr wollt**
Sie sollen	**Sie sollen**	**Sie wollen**	**Sie wollen**
er		**er**	
sie soll	**sie sollen**	**sie will**	**sie wollen**
es		**es**	

1. **Was soll ich trinken?**
2. **Du willst vielleicht Milch.**
3. **Das kannst Du trinken.**
4. **Ich will lieber Schnaps.**

möchten (should) would like

ich möchte	**wir möchten**
du möchtest	**ihr möchtet**
Sie möchten	**Sie möchten**
er, sie, es möchte	**sie möchten**

'möchten' (like all other modal verbs) is not followed by 'zu'
It is a term used a lot to indicate what you would or would not like (to)...

In English one would say: 'I would (should) like **to** go'.
In German you would say: **'Ich möchte gehen'.**

Ich möchte ein Bier trinken.

Ich möchte gern ein Bier trinken.
Ich möchte lieber eine Limonade trinken.
Ich möchte am liebsten ein Glas Wein trinken.
(See previous chapter, p.59: 'gern', 'lieber', am 'liebsten'.)

Ich möchte kein Bier.
Ich möchte nicht gern Bier trinken.

Verb practice:

Write out all the present tense forms of 'sagen', 'machen', 'gehen' 'fahren', 'besuchen', 'nehmen'.

Look up: Present tense, p.191 and vowel change for 'nehmen' in the list of irregular verbs, 2nd column.

Translate:

you are saying (all forms).
I am visiting
we are going
he/she is driving
they are speaking
you are making (all forms)
we are eating
she drives
we make
he comes

Verb practice ctd.:

Separable verbs:	anrufen, freinehmen, kennenlernen, wegfahren, ansehen (to look at) Ich lern- Berlin k-----. Du fähr-- jetzt w--. Er ruf- gleich a-. Ich nehm- einenTag f---. Wir seh-- das Buch a-.
Sep. verbs and modals:	Ich (wollen) Wien kennenlernen. Du (müssen) jetzt wegfahren. Er (können) gleich anrufen. Sie (sollen) uns mitnehmen. (mitnehmen to take somebody with you) Ihr (möchten) heute zurückkommen. (möchten zurückkommen would like to come back)
'möchten':	When would you like to come? We would very much like to come in summer. He would like a glass of wine. They would rather see the mountains. We would rather not eat Sauerkraut. (lieber rather)

Write out a dialogue similar to the one you have just read on p.63, arranging a trip with friends. Read it out aloud.

Include: destination, suggest duration, when to depart, arrive and return, mode of transport. Can you make it? Yes/no. Give reasons. Useful words: 'wo', 'wohin', 'wann'.

Pairwork:
Ask one another questions on the topic 'trips, short breaks': Wohin fahren Sie manchmal? Wann? Wie? Wer bleibt zu Haus? etc.

- **Booking hotel accommodation** A phone conversation

Herr Müller kennt ein nettes Hotel in Wien. Er telefoniert mit der Inhaberin.

Frau Riedl: Hotel Zentrum, guten Tag (Grüß Gott).

Herr Müller: **Hallo Frau Riedl, hier Fritz Müller** aus Frankfurt.

Frau Riedl: Ach ja, **Herr Müller, wie geht's?**

Herr Müller: **Sehr gut, danke, und Ihnen?**

Frau Riedl: **Recht gut, danke, immer viel zu tun.**

Herr Müller: Frau Riedl, **wir möchten gern wieder nach Wien kommen. Haben Sie noch Zimmer frei?**

Frau Riedl: **Wann wollen Sie kommen?**

Herr Müller: Nächstes Wochenende.
Haben Sie vielleicht ein Doppelzimmer für mich und meine Frau und ein Einzelzimmer für meinen Kollegen.

Frau Riedl: **Für wie lange?**

Herr Müller: **Für drei Nächte.** Freitag, Samstag (Sonnabend), und Sonntag.

Frau Riedl: Sie haben Glück. **Wir haben die gewünschten Zimmer. Mit Bad und Dusche.**

Herr Müller: **Und was kosten die Zimmer?**

Frau Riedl: **Das Doppelzimmer kostet 1000 Schilling, das Einzelzimmer 800 Schilling pro Übernachtung und Frühstück.**

Herr Müller: Gut. **Können Sie bitte beide Zimmer reservieren?**

Frau Riedl: Ja, gern. **Ich freue mich, daß Sie wieder kommen.**

Herr Müller: **Auf Wiederhören, bis Freitag.**

Frau Riedl: **Auf Wiederhören und schönen Gruß an Frau Müller.**

Kennen Sie ein nettes Hotel? Wo? Buchen Sie einen Urlaub für sich und ...

der(die) Inhaber(in)	owner(f.)	**kennen**	to know
die Nacht(¨e)	night	**telefonieren**	to phone
das Frühstück	breakfast	**reservieren**	to reserve
		möchten	would like
das Zimmer(-)	room	**kosten**	to cost
das Einzelzimmer	single room		
das Doppelzimmer	double room	**gewünscht**	desired
		frei	free
der Samstag	Saturday		
der Sonnabend	Saturday (North Germany)	**nächst**	next
der Sonntag	Sunday	**beide**	both

(see p.148-149 for more information on indications of time)

der Schilling	Austrian currency

Hallo!	Hello!
Sie haben Glück!	you are lucky
Auf Wiederhören!	Good-bye! (phone)
Schönen Gruß!	Remember me to.. (greetings and best wishes)

(Phone vocabulary - appendix, p.167)

- **Booking rooms, making reservations etc.:**

For information on accommodation contact the local tourist-office **(Fremdenverkehrsamt)** or the National Tourist Offices of Germany, Austria and Switzerland.

das Hotel(s)	hotel
das Hotel garni	room and breakfast only
die Pension(en)	Usually very pleasant, family run establishments offering good value. And you don't have to be out by 10 o'clock!
die Frühstückspension	same as above
die Raststätte, der Rasthof	Motel, usually just off the motorway or main routes.
die Ferienwohnung(en)	holiday apartment
Vollpension	full board
Halbpension	half board
Zimmer frei	rooms free, vacancies

Signs by the roadside will make it easy for you to find accommodation when travelling. This is particularly true in holiday areas.

Fremdenzimmer zu vermieten	rooms to let

Haben Sie Zimmer frei?	Are there any vacancies?
Für wie viele Personen?	For how many people?
Für wie lange?	For how long?
Was kostet/kosten ....?	How much is ....?
Ich (wir) möchte(n) ein Zimmer reservieren	I (we) would like to reserve a room
das Einzelzimmer/Doppelzimmer	single/double room*
	* usually twin bedded
mit WC/Toilette	with toilet
mit Bad/Dusche	with bath/shower
mit Telefon/Fernseher	with telephone/television
Übernachtung mit Frühstück	bed and breakfast
pro Nacht/proTag	per night/per day
inklusive Mehrwertsteuer	V.A.T. included
Bedienung	service charge
der Schlüssel(n)	key

If equipment does not work:	**die Dusche funktioniert nicht**
If something is broken:	**die Lampe ist kaputt**
kaputt	means just that something needs repairing
total kaputt	beyond repair, a write off

- **Filling in the registration form:**

It is a requirement to register after more than three days in any one place, you may be handed a form, the **'Anmeldeschein'** or **'Meldezettel'**, at the reception **(Empfang)** in your hotel and asked to fill it in.

Bitte füllen Sie den Meldezettel aus und unterschreiben Sie hier!
Please, fill out this registration form and sign here.

ausfüllen(s.)	to fill out	**unterschreiben**	to sign
der Wohnort	place of residence	**der Geburtsort**	place of birth
das Geburtsdatum	date of birth	**der Beruf(e)**	profession, job

letzter Aufenthaltsort/Reiseziel	last place of your stay/destination
die Kraftfahrzeugnummer(n)	vehicle registration number
die Staatszugehörigkeit	nationality

Pretend you are dictating your particulars to the receptionist **(Empfangsdame)** filling out a registration form for you. Speak in sentences. Mein Wohnort ist.......etc.

Hotel Zentrum

Exercises as on p.41 and p.52 but within the context of this picture.

CHAPTER 8

In Wien *In Vienna*

- Was machen wir heute? (What shall we do today?)
- At Breakfast. Shopping. At the Bank.
- Present tense implying the future. Accusative with direction.
- Prepositions taking dative or accusative. 'Dürfen'.
- Genitive, genitive prepositions.

- **Beim Frühstück im Hotel Zentrum** At breakfast at the hotel Zentrum

Frau Riedel: **Guten Morgen! Gut geschlafen?**

Herr Müller: **Sehr gut, danke.** Wir waren sehr müde.

Frau Riedel: **Was möchten Sie zum Frühstück, meine Herrschaften?**

Frau Müller: Was gibt es denn?

Frau Riedel: **Es gibt kaltes Buffet: Schinken, Wurst und Käse. Verschiedene Brotsorten, Brötchen oder Semmeln,** wie man in Wien sagt. Hier im Körbchen ist frisches Gebäck.
Mehrere Sorten Marmelade, Honig und Joghurt.

John: Gibt es auch Eier? Ich möchte gern **ein weiches (weichgekochtes) Ei,** bitte nicht **ein hartes (hartgekochtes) Ei.**

Frau Riedel: Gern. Zu trinken gibt es **Kaffee, Tee, Kakao, Schokolade, Milch oder Kräutertee, was Sie wollen.**

Frau Müller: Die Auswahl ist ja sehr groß, aber ich darf nicht zu viel essen.
Einen Pfefferminztee mit Zitrone und Früchtejoghurt mit Honig, bitte.

Herr Müller: Du machst schon wieder Hungerdiät! Ich aber nicht!
Ich möchte lieber Aufschnitt, Semmeln und starken Kaffee.

John: **Am liebsten hätte ich ein Kännchen Tee mit Milch. Müsli und ein weiches Ei, bitte.**

Sie sind in einem Hotel. Bestellen Sie Frühstück für sich und Ihre Familie. See p.73

gut geschlafen	(Have you) slept well?
wir waren	we were
müde	tired

Meine Herrschaften! Ladies and Gentlemen! A polite way of addressing customers.

das Buffet	buffet	**die Marmelade(n)**	jam
die Sorte(n)	sort, type	**die Orangenmarmelade**	marmalade
das Brötchen(-)	bread roll		
die Semmel(n)	bread roll (Austria)	**der Honig**	honey
das Gebäck	coll. noun for different types of rolls	**der Joghurt**	yogurt
		das Ei(er)	egg
		weich(gekocht)	soft(boiled)
das Körbchen	small basket	**hart(gekocht)**	hard(boiled)
der Tee(s)	tea	**der Kaffee(s)**	coffee
der Kräutertee	herb tea	**der Kakao**	cocoa
Pfefferminztee	peppermint tea	**die Schokolade(n)**	chocolate
die Zitrone(n)	lemon	**der Aufschnitt**	selection of cold meats
die Frucht(¨e)	fruit		
das Kännchen Tee/Kaffee	pot of tea/coffee	**das Müsli**	muesli

die Diät(en)	diet	**die Auswahl**	choice
die Hungerdiät	starvation diet		
Diät machen	to (be) go on a diet		
frisch	fresh	**mehrere**	several

Was möchten Sie zum Frühstück?	What would you like for breakfast?
Ich möchte/wir möchten (gern) ...	I/we would like ...
Ich hätte gern ...	I should/would like ...
das ist mir am liebsten	I like that best

'dürfen' to be allowed to', 'may' (modal verb)

ich darf	(I am allowed, I may)	**wir dürfen**	**Darf ich hier parken?**
du darfst		**ihr dürft**	May I park here?
Sie dürfen		**Sie dürfen**	
er			No, you **must not** park here.
sie darf		**sie dürfen**	**Nein, Sie dürfen hier nicht parken.**
es			

'must not' is expressed by forms of **'dürfen' + 'nicht'**

Exercises: Further to 'Breakfast'

Express your likes and preferences as well as dislikes of certain breakfast foods.

Pretend you are talking to a companion over breakfast. If in a classroom situation, talk to your neighbour:

Ask him/her what he/she would like to eat and drink. Offer a choice. Use the 'Sie' and 'Du' forms of 'möchten' und 'wollen'.

- **Was machen wir heute?** What shall we do today?

John: *(after breakfast)* **Was machen wir heute vormittag?**

Herr Müller: **Wir beginnen mit einem Rundgang im Zentrum Wiens**, da gibt es genug zu sehen.

John: Gibt es auch elegante Geschäfte, **ich möchte nämlich einkaufen gehen.**

Herr Müller: **Haben Sie ein dickes Scheckbuch, Kreditkarte und viel Geld mit?**

John: *(smiling, tongue in cheek)* Kein Problem. Sie wissen doch, mein Chef ist sehr großzügig.

Herr Müller: *(grinning)* Wirklich? Das ist ja gut, wenn man so ein Glück hat.

John: Können wir auch in den Dom gehen? In dem alten Gebäude gibt es sicher viel Interessantes zu sehen.

Frau Müller: Aber bitte nicht die vielen Stufen auf den Turm steigen! Dazu habe ich nicht genug Energie.

Herr Müller: Kein Wunder, Du ißt zu wenig. Deine Figur ist für dich wichtiger als Kultur.

Von oben hat man einen wunderbaren Ausblick auf die Stadt, ihre Umgebung und die blaue Donau.

Frau Müller: Seit wann ist Treppensteigen Kultur? Außerdem ist die Donau selten blau.

John: **Zuerst muß ich ein paar Geschenke kaufen. Hier ist eine Konditorei. Da gibt es sicher exklusive Schokoladen.**

der Rundgang(¨e)	a walk round	**machen**	to do
		beginnen	to begin
das Scheckbuch(¨er)	cheque-book	**sehen**	to see
die Kreditkarte(n)	credit card		
das Geld(er)	money	**einkaufen(s.)**	to shop
		gehen	to go
das Geschenk(e)	present	**kaufen**	to buy
der Dom(e)	cathedral		
die Stufe(n)	step		
der Turm(¨e)	tower, spire	**steigen**	to climb
die Energie(n)	energy	**essen**	to eat
das Wunder(-)	wonder, miracle	(du ißt)	
die Figur(en)	figure		
die Kultur(en)	culture	**mithaben(s.)**	to have with you
der Ausblick(e)	view		
die Umgebung(en)	surroundings	**wissen**	to know
die Treppe(n)	stairs	(irreg. verb	see list, p.202)
die Donau	Danube		
die Konditorei(n)	cake shop (exquisite cakes and chocolates)		
vormittag	(late) morning ca. 10 to 12 o'clock	**nämlich**	namely (filler word), don't translate
heute	today	**dick**	thick, fat
heute vormittag	this morning	**großzügig**	generous
Glück haben	to be lucky	**wirklich**	really
		wenig	little (amounts)
so ein ...	such a ...		
		wichtig	important
viel Interessantes	much of interest	**für dich**	for you
seit wann	since when		
zuerst	first of all	**von oben**	from above
		außerdem	besides
selten	rarely	**sicher**	for sure
exklusiv	exclusive	**ein paar**	a few

The present tense often conveys the future:

Ich komme in drei Tagen. I am coming (I shall, I am going to come) in three days.
Was machen wir heute? What are we going to do?

The following prepositions can be followed either by the Accusative or Dative:

ACCUSATIVE	**in** (in) **auf** (on) **an** (at) **neben** (next to)
	vor(in front of) **hinter** (at the back of)
When movement (→) is implied:	**unter** (under) **ober** (above) **über** (above) **zwischen** (between)
	Der Mann geht **in den** (**einen**) Garten. (The man goes → into the (a) garden.) (See also: Chapter 5)
DATIVE	
When no movement is implied:	Der Mann sitzt **in dem** (**einem**) Garten. (The man sits in the garden.)

As you won't yet know the pattern of cases and related endings, you will need to consult your table of cases in the Grammar Summary for the next exercise. Noun genders are shown in brackets to make your task easier.

Remember, when **'in'** (in) and **'on'** (auf) become directional in meaning ('into' and 'onto'), you need the accusative case.

Exercise:

Ich stehe auf d-- hoh-- Turm. (m.)
Ich steige auf d-- hoh-- Turm.

Wir sind in d-- alt-- Stadt. (f.)
Wir fahren in d-- alt-- Stadt.

Sie ist in d-- interessant-- Museum. (n)
Sie geht in d-- interessant- Museum.

Having worked out all the endings you might well ask, however do Germans cope with this aspect of their language?

The simple answer is that one's native language is basically absorbed in chunks of speech, mirroring concepts. You would automatically say e.g. 'mit dem Bus' or 'in dem Haus' rather than 'mit der Bus' and 'in das Haus' because that is what you would have heard repeatedly in this context if you were constantly surrounded by German speakers.

When learning a second language, however, it is necessary to first of all build up a collection of words and short phrases as one's memory cannot cope with more at that stage.

As your brain gets flooded with more German, you too will begin to think in bigger units, with the right grammar built in as it were. Eventually you will have automatic recall of quite a lot of the new language, it builds up gradually.

Only retrospectively, e.g. when learning as an adult, does one need analysis to explain why certain things are the way they are.

However, having taken on board all about the changes prevously explained, you can relax again. Nobody expects you to get these things right when you are using your newly acquired knowledge of German. Say what you want to say, when you want to say it, Germans will correct you occasionally in an effort to help. Incidentally, they too make case mistakes as the language spoken in the various regions often deviates quite a bit from the norms of standard German.

- **John kauft Geschenke** John buys presents

- Shopping: The reference section in the appendix contains information on all aspects of shopping. Types of shops, stores, products, sizes, weights, measures, colours and money.

John confidently buys expensive chocolates in one of Vienna's exclusive patisserie shops. Money is no object until he realises his credit card is a day out of date.

John: Guten Tag! *(It is customary to greet when entering a shop.)*

Assistant: Grüß Gott! Bitte schön?

John: **Ich möchte Geschenke kaufen,** für meine Familie und Kollegen in England. Die Auswahl hier ist ja fantastisch!

Assistant: **Ja, wir verkaufen sehr viele verschiedene Sorten Schokoladen und Pralinen. Wieviel wollen Sie denn ausgeben?**

John: Das spielt keine Rolle, **ich zahle mit Kreditkarte. Ich nehme zwei große Schachteln Pralinen,** diese hier vorne links und **drei kleine Schachteln,** da hinten rechts. **Auch zehn Tafeln Schokolade von dieser Spezialmarke. Ich glaube, das ist alles.**

Assistant: Soll ich alles hübsch verpacken und nach England schicken?

John: Gute Idee! Dann nehme ich noch eine Sachertorte.
(A very special Viennese chocolate cake, frequently dispatched to the far corners of the earth. Very expensive!)

Assistant: **Ist das alles?** Welches Geschenkpapier hätten Sie gern?
Dieses ist recht hübsch.

John: **Ja, bitte. Das gefällt mir sehr gut. Wunderbar!**
Was kostet das alles?

Assistant: Das macht 1200S. *(Quite a high price!)*

John: *(stops himself from fainting on the spot)* **Hier ist meine Karte.**

Assistant: *(looks at the expiry date)* **Leider nicht mehr gültig, sie ist gestern abgelaufen.**

John: **Entschuldigen Sie bitte, das ist mir sehr peinlich!**
Ich zahle bar, muß aber schnell zuerst zur Bank.

die Sorte(n)	sort, type	**verkaufen**	to sell
die Praline(n)	filled chocolates	**ausgeben(s.)**	to spend
die Tafel Schokolade	bar of chocolate	**zahlen (bar)**	to pay (in cash)
die Auswahl	choice	**kosten**	to cost
die Schachtel(n)	box	**glauben**	to think, believe
die Spezialmarke(n)	special brand		
das Geschenkpapier(e)	wrapping paper	**schicken**	to send

noch	still, in addition, else	**gültig**	valid
das spielt keine Rolle	that does not matter	**gestern**	yesterday
nicht mehr gültig	not valid any more	**ist abgelaufen**	has run out
das ist mir sehr peinlich	this is very embarrassing		

das gefällt mir (sehr gut) I like that (a lot)
'gefallen' + dative very often conveys visual or aesthetic appreciation.

Was hätten Sie gern?	What would you like?	**Ist das alles?**	Is that all?
Ich hätte gern...	I would like ...	**Das ist alles.**	That is all.
('möchten ' is another option)			
Was kostet... ?	What is the cost of ...?	**Das macht..**	That comes to
Ich zahle bar.	I am paying cash..		

LET'S PRACTISE SHOPPING

The verbs you are most likely to use:		
	möchten	would like
	hätte gern	ditto
	wollen	to want
	haben	to have
	brauchen	to need

Remember to use the accusative as anything you would like, want, need etc. is an object:

Ich möchte (and now the object) ein**en** warm**en** Pullover (m.)*
eine weiße Bluse (f.)
ein rotes Hemd (n.)

* The endings only change with masculine nouns.
(See chapter 5, p.48 or the case table in the appendix, p.197.)

Shopping for clothes

Exercise: Choose five items of clothing from the section 'Clothes' in the appendix, p.150-151 and pretend you are asking for them in a shop.

Pair-work: Discuss what clothes you need for a summer holiday and a skiing trip.

Take turns in being the shop assistent or customer, make rough notes and refer to them if necessary. Try to face the person you are speaking to. Grammar is of secondary importance here as this is an exercise to promote oral skills.

Don't forget colours (appendix, p.150-151), sizes and any details you think are important, your tutor will help if necessary.

Expressing likes and dislikes:
(as in visual sense, see also p.163)

Diese Farbe (colour) **gefällt mir (nicht)**.
Diese Schuhe **gefallen mir (nicht).**
Ich finde den Bikini schön/nicht schön.

Shopping for food

Prepare dialogues in groups or pairs (see above):
You are shopping for a barbecue.
You are expecting guests for dinner.
(See appendix, p.152-157: Food, weights, measures.)
Tell the story of John's shopping efforts in a few short sentences. Use the present tense.

- **In der Bank** At the Bank

John braucht dringend Geld — John needs money urgently

Unable to pay for his expensive presents he rushes round the corner to the bank only to find it closed. He reads the notice on opening times. (These vary, so it is best to have a look at the beginning of your stay before you are in financial despair.)

Geschäftsstunden hours of business **geöffnet** open **geschlossen** closed

John: Wie dumm, die Bank ist noch zu!

Austrian: Haben Sie es sehr eilig?

John: Ja, ich brauche dringend Bargeld für meine Einkäufe. **Meine Kreditkarte ist nicht mehr gültig. Sie ist gestern abgelaufen.**

Austrian: *(nodding sympathetically)* Leider ist Wien nicht billig.

John: *(thinking of his expensive purchases)* Das kann man wohl sagen.

Wie dumm!	How annoying! How silly!	**das Bargeld**	cash
Die Bank ist noch zu.	The bank is still closed.	**der Einkauf(¨e)**	purchase
Haben Sie es eilig?	Are you in a hurry?	**dringend**	urgently

Das kann man wohl sagen. You can say that again.

(a little later inside the bank)

Official: Bitte schön?

John: **Ich möchte 5 Reiseschecks zu 50 Pfund einlösen.**

Official: **Bitte unterschreiben Sie die Schecks. Ihren Paß, bitte.**

John: Wo ist der nur? *(frantically feeling his pockets)*
Hoffentlich nicht im Hotel. *(But he is lucky for once.)*
Bitte schön, mein Paß.

Official: Sie haben Glück, der Kurs ist heute sehr günstig.
Sie bekommen ...Schilling und ...Groschen.
(1 Schilling = 100 Groschen)
(In Deutschland: 1 Mark = 100 Pfennige)

John:	**Bitte hauptsächlich Geldscheine. Ich habe genug Münzen und Kleingeld.**
Official:	*(handing John a chit)* **Hier ist Ihr Kassenzettel, bitte gehen Sie damit zur Kassa da drüben. Dort bekommen Sie das Geld.**

In addition to being called 'Bank' you will find a variety of names for banks such as Sparkasse (savings-bank), Creditanstalt, Bankverein, Landesbank to name just a few.

There is a very comprehensive list of banking and financial terms on page 176.

der Scheck(s)	cheque	**der Geldschein(e)**	bank note
der Wechselkurs(e)	exchange rate	**die Münze(n)**	coin
		das Kleingeld	change
bekommen	to get, receive	**die Kassa(Kassen)**	till, cash desk
wechseln	to change	**der Zettel(-)**	receipt, chit
günstig	favourable, good		
einen Reisescheck einlösen	to cash a traveller's cheque		
Wie ist der Kurs heute?	What is the rate today?		

Exercise: Ask for x amounts of pounds to be changed into marks.
Ask what the exchange rate is today.
Say, you would like to transfer x amounts of money to England.
Ask: Is it cheaper to change money at (in) a bank or a bureau de change.

('Banking and Finance' terminology, p.176 for words you have not met)

Welche Fragen stellen Sie manchmal in Ihrer Bank?
(Fragen stellen	to ask questions)

What is my balance?
Can I draw x amounts of Pounds, Marks, Francs, Shillings?
Is it possible to order x amounts of ... (any foreign currency).
What is the rate today?

('Banking and Finance' terminology, p.176)

Genitive or Possessive Case

The last case we have to deal with, it is mostly translated by 'of the', 'of a'.

(The articles change in the way shown below)

das Buch

des jungen Mannes (m.)	**der** deutschen Frau (f.)	**des** kleinen Kindes (n.)
eines jungen Mannes	**einer** deutschen Frau	**eines** kleinen Kindes

the book

of the(a) young man	of the(a) German woman	of the(a) small child
the(a) young man's book	the(a) German woman's b.	the small child's book

The Genitive is also always used after:

(an)statt instead of **trotz** inspite of **wegen** because of **während** during **hinsichtlich** in view of **bezüglich** referring to

Table of Cases: p.197

Genitive exercises:
the tower of the(a) cathedral, the centre of the(a) town, the garden of the(a) house
Look at one of the large pictures and pick out three examples using the Genitive: e.g. the window of the shop, the spire of the church etc.

Translate:		
	in spite of the winter	(der Winter)
	during the week	(die Woche)
	because of the wind	(der Wind)
	instead of a car	(das Auto)
	during a concert	(das Konzert)

CHAPTER 9

Mittagessen mit Sabine *Lunch with Sabine*

- John sets out on his own in search of a pleasant restaurant. He is soon given friendly advice by Sabine, a pleasant Viennese student.

- Asking for and giving directions.
- The polite way of issuing, accepting or refusing invitations.
- Imperative. Dative verbs. Reflexive verbs.
- 'to', the differences between 'zu' and 'nach'.

Mittagszeit, ein heißer Tag in Wien Lunchtime, a hot day inVienna

Frau Müller: Es ist heute schrecklich heiß und ich bin eigentlich sehr müde.

Herr Müller: Essen wir lieber abends statt zu Mittag, ich habe noch keinen Hunger.

Frau Müller: Prima, ich bin auch dafür. Ich möchte mich ein bißchen im Hotel ausruhen.

John: Das macht nichts, ich finde sicher ein nettes Restaurant, ich habe schon Hunger. Wir treffen uns später und gehen dann aus.

schrecklich	terrible	**heiß**	hot
müde	tired	**ein bißchen**	a bit
		eigentlich	actually
abends	in the evening	**spät**	late
am Abend	ditto	**nett**	nice
zu Mittag	at lunchtime	**(an)statt**	instead
(see appendix: p.149, times of the day)		**finden**	to find
		sich ausruhen(r.)+	to have a rest

ich bin dafür*	I am on for that, I agree	**sich treffen(r.)+**	to meet
das macht nichts	that does not matter	(+ reflexive verbs, see p.190)	
(* see overleaf)		**ausgehen(s.)**	to go out

ich habe Hunger (Durst)	I am hungry (thursty)
ich habe (noch) keinen Hunger (Durst)	I am not (yet) hungry (thursty)

Exercise:	Kennen Sie ein gutes Restaurant? Gehen Sie manchmal aus? Wann? Wo? Wie oft? Allein?

*** There are quite a few word combinations like:**

dafür for that **damit** with that **davon** from/of that **davor** in front of that
darunter under that **darüber** over that **dahinter** behind that etc.

The 'da'-part stands for 'das' (that) not for 'da' meaning 'here'.

- **Wo ist hier ein gutes Restaurant?** Where is there a good restaurant?

John: *(Standing on the pavement, looking round, consulting his guide book and map. A friendly-looking young lady is about to pass him)*

Entschuldigen Sie bitte, vielleicht können Sie mir helfen?
Kennen Sie hier in der Nähe ein nettes Restaurant?

Sabine: **Doch, weiter vorn ist ein gutes Restaurant, das Gasthaus 'Zum goldenen Löwen'.**

John: Ist das weit?

Sabine: Nein, kommen Sie, ich zeige es Ihnen.
Wir gehen nur zirka 100m (Meter) geradeaus bis zur Kreuzung.
Sind Sie Engländer? Sie sprechen gut Deutsch.

John: Mein Deutsch ist leider nie gut genug für die Speisekarte.
Besonders hier in Österreich.

Sabine: Das kann ich verstehen. Sehen Sie, hier ist das Gasthaus.
Man kann auch draußen sitzen, ein paar Tische sind noch frei.

John: Vielleicht können Sie mir mit der Speisekarte helfen.
Darf ich Sie zum Mittagessen einladen?

Sabine: Aber sie kennen mich doch nicht! **Das ist aber nett von Ihnen.**
Danke, Herr...?

John: Peters, John Peters.
Nichts zu danken, es ist mir ein Vergnügen, Fräulein ...?

Sabine: Eger, Sabine Eger *(shaking hands with John)*. Ich muß sagen, auch ich bin schon hungrig. Es ist ja schon Mittagszeit.

das Gasthaus(¨er)	pub/restaurant	**das Mittagessen**	lunch
die Speisekarte(n)	menu	**die Mittagszeit(en)**	lunchtime

weit	far	**besonders**	particularly
draußen	outside	**frei**	free
der Löwe(n)	lion	**hungrig**	hungry
die Kreuzung(en)	crossroads	**nie**	never
		gut genug	good enough
der Tisch(e)	table		
das Vergnügen	pleasure	**einladen**	to invite
		sitzen	to sit
weiter vorn	further on	**helfen***	to help
geradeaus	straight on	**zeigen***	to show
		danken*	to thank

Dative Verbs

'helfen', 'zeigen', 'danken', 'sagen' are followed by the dative.

Sie helfen **mir** (dative of 'ich')
Wir danken **dem jungen Mann**

Ich helfe **Ihnen** (dative of 'Sie')
Wir danken **ihm** (dative of 'er')

Er zeigt **ihm** den Park, die Stadt, das Haus. (The dative comes before the accusative.)
D. A.

Pronouns and their Cases

	sg.						pl.			
	I	you*	you+	he	she	it	we	you*	you+	they
Nom.	**ich**	**du**	**Sie**	**er**	**sie**	**es**	**wir**	**ihr**	**Sie**	**sie**
Acc.	**mich**	**dich**	**Sie**	**ihn**	**sie**	**es**	**uns**	**euch**	**Sie**	**sie**
Dat.	**mir**	**dir**	**Ihnen**	**ihm**	**ihr**	**ihm**	**uns**	**euch**	**Ihnen**	**Ihnen**

* familiar + polite

Exercises:	Turn to page 197 in the appendix showing all the prepositions and their cases, choose prepositions and convert five nominative pronoun forms (p.85) to the cases the prepositions require. Translate: from us, near them, after him, to me, to you (all forms), with you (pol.), through us, against her, on it, in it. Team up three prepositions from each one of the groups shown below (for a summary look at p.197, bottom of page) with pronouns from the box on p.85. accusative prepositions, dative prepositions, dative/acc. prepositions e.g. von mir (from me), mit Ihnen (with you), durch ihn (through him) etc.

Now for a bit of light relief let me tell you a little about cultural differences when it comes to invitations, food and eating.

• Dos and Don'ts when socialising •

Invitations Always bring flowers, chocolates or both. Unwrap the flowers before handing them to the hostess. (This is usually done just before the door is opened. Yes, really!)

Don't bring red roses, if you don't want to end up in an embarrassing situation since they are a symbol of love.

Don't bring a bottle of wine! It is a bit like bringing your own bottle of milk to a coffee morning. Moreover they are in a position to buy better quality wines at lower prices and are quite knowledgeble on the subject.

Written 'thank you' notes are not necessary, phone calls will do equally well.

Do dress reasonably well! 'Down dressing' might be fine with some younger folk but is not the norm in business and professional circles or the mainstream of German society. In some respects though German people dress less formally than their English counter parts e.g. during hot weather, at most weddings (no crazy hats, rarely morning suits) or at school (no uniforms!). I am afraid, people tend to be judged by their appearances. Slight dottiness and neglect of one's personal attire is not met with the same amused tolerance as is the case in Britain.

Food	On the whole German people like a substantial warm meal once a day, very often at lunchtime. They eat more meat and savoury things than in England. Desserts are not a great priority. On the whole cakes etc. are for special occasions or when going out having coffee. They like to eat quality food and don't regard snacking as a very good idea.
	Terminology for food, meals, drinks etc. varies quite a lot in German speaking countries. There is a fairly comprehensive list of food items and related vocabulary in the appendix from p.152 onwards.
At the table	Don't keep your hands under the table, rest them lightly on the edge of the table or on your lap.
	There are a number of foods where Germans will use a fork only (in the right hand).These are soft foods such as egg dishes which do not need a knife.
	It is not considered impolite to talk while eating. Germans and Austrians particularly love a good exchange of ideas at all times. To show friendly interest in what you do etc. is regarded as normal although you might occasionally think it intrusive.

- **Invitations:**

Darf ich Sie zum Mittagessen oder Abendessen einladen?	May I invite you for lunch or dinner?
Danke, gern. Das ist sehr nett von Ihnen.	Thank you. That is very kind of you.
Nichts zu danken.	Don't mention it.
Es ist mir ein Vergnügen.	It is a pleasure.
Leider kann ich nicht kommen.	I can't come, unfortunately.
Es geht leider nicht.	I am sorry, it is not possible
Geht es vielleicht ein anderes Mal?	Perhaps another time?
Haben Sie meine Adresse?	Have you got my address?
Bitte, geben Sie mir Ihre Telefonnummer.	Please, let me have your phone number.

Exercises: Put into German:

May we invite you to dinner?
Many thanks. At what time? (When?)
At 7 o'clock.Where do you live?
Here is my address: e.g. Goethe Straße, zweiter Stock, Tür Nummer 3.*
Have I (got) your phone number?
* der Stock(¨e) floor, numbers p.147

Dialogues (Pair work):

Issue invitations to one another. Specify the occasion, time of arrival and place.
Exchange phone numbers and addresses.
Respond using the phrases above by accepting.
Alternatively apologize and give a reason why you can't come.

Discuss what you want to do, where you would like to go etc. using 'wollen' and 'möchten'.

Exchange opinions on arranging a 'do':
What do you think? What should we do etc.?
A party, a lunch or dinner to celebrate ...?

der Geburtstag(e) birthday **die Feier(n)** celebration **das Jubiläum** anniversary **der Hochzeitstag(e)** wedding anniversary

In the dialogue at the beginning of this chapter we came across two reflexive verbs:

sich ausruhen	to have a rest	**sich treffen**	to meet

Reflexive Verb Pattern
(see p.190)

sich interessieren (für) to be interested (in)

ich interessiere			**mich**	**wir interessieren**			**uns**
du	**"**	**st**	**dich**	**ihr**	**"**	**t**	**euch**
Sie	**"**	**en**	**sich**	**Sie**	**"**	**en**	**sich**
er **sie** **es**	**"**	**t**	**sich**	**sie**	**"**	**en**	**sich**

sich waschen	to wash	**sich rasieren**	to shave
sich anziehen(s.)	to dress	**sich ausziehen(s.)**	to undress
sich freuen auf...	to look forward to...	**sich freuen über...**	to be pleased about...

Translate: I am pleased about the present. I look forward to the summer.
I must have a wash now. He should shave in the morning.

Answer: Interessieren sie sich für Musik?
Treffen Sie sich oft mit Freunden?
Worauf (auf was)(*) freuen Sie sich?
Worüber (über was)(*) freuen Sie sich?

(*) **Contractions of prepositions and 'wo'.** These are quite common
(The 'wo'- part stands for 'was', not 'where'.)

Wofür, woraus, womit, worauf and worüber: Can you guess their meaning?

Exceptions: **'wohin'** where to **'woher'** where from

- **Sabine gives directions to a tourist** (Key phrases)

Sabine: *(sees an elderly gentleman trying to make sense of his map)*
Einen Augenblick, John! *(turns to the tourist)*

Kann ich Ihnen helfen? Wohin wollen Sie denn?

Tourist: **Ich möchte zum Kohlmarkt. Können Sie mir sagen, wo wir sind? Ich weiß es leider nicht.**

Sabine: **Wir sind auf dem Albertinaplatz. Gehen Sie hier links und geradeaus die Augustinerstraße entlang. Dann kommen Sie zu einem Durchgang in den Michaelerplatz. Danach rechts um die Ecke und Sie sind am Kohlmarkt.**

Tourist: **Herzlichen Dank! Auf Wiedersehen!**

der Durchgang	passage	**um die Ecke**	round the corner
entlang	along	**geradeaus**	straight on

- **Asking the way:**

Entschuldigen Sie, bitte!	Excuse me please?
Können Sie mir helfen?	Can you help me ?
Wo ist ...?	Where is ...?
Wie komme ich ...?	How do I get to ...?
Wie fahre ich ...?	How do I drive to ...?
Wie gehe ich am besten zu ...?	What is the best way to ...? How do I go best to ...?

'to' **zu:** Wie komme ich **zum Park, zur Kirche zum Hotel?**

nach: With named geographical locations. Ich fahre **nach** Berlin.

There is one exeption: Wir gehen **nach Haus.** (We are going home.)

- **Giving directions:**

Gehen Sie ...	Go ...	**geradeaus**	straight on
Fahren Sie ...	Drive ...	**links, rechts**	to the left, to the right
(See 'Imperative'.)			
entlang	along	**danach**	after that
die Straße entlang	along the road	**um die Ecke**	round the corner
die Straße hoch (hinauf)	up the road	**in Richtung**	in the direction
bis	until, up to	**der Eingang(¨e)**	entrance
bis zur Kreuzung	to the crossroads	**der Ausgang(¨e)**	exit
bis zur Ampel	to the traffic lights	**der Kreisverkehr**	roundabout

Sie müssen links/rechts abbiegen.	You have to turn off to the left/right.
Sie müssen die Straße überqueren.	You have to cross the road.
Sie müssen (hier) halten.	You have to stop (here).
50 Meter weiter	50 metres further on

Exercise:	You have missed your last train/tram/bus. Ask someone to direct you to the nearest taxi rank. Give the driver instructions on how to reach your hotel. (See 'Imperative', 'Sie' form on page 91.) How do you get to your nearest post office, shopping centre, church, railway station or any place of your choice? (Choose two examples)

The Imperative or command form

If you wanted to tell someone to do something e.g. to go or to drive you would say:

Go straight on! **Drive** round the corner!

In German you add a 'Sie' for the polite form:

Gehen Sie links!	**Fahren Sie** um die Ecke!	**'Sie' form (sg. and pl.)**
Geh geradeaus!	**Fahr** um die Ecke!	**'Du' form no ending (sg.)**
Geht geradeaus!	**Fahrt** um die Ecke!	**'t' ending (pl.)**

Vowel changes in the 'Du' form are frequently found in verbs with 'e' stem vowel

sprechen	Sprich!	sehen	Sieh!	essen	Iß!

- **Modal verbs on their own:**

In the previous dialogue we have two examples of what seems like an incomplete sentence:

Wohin wollen Sie denn?	Where do you want to go (then)?
Ich möchte zum Kohlmarkt.	I would like to go to the Kohlmarkt
Ich muß schnell zur Bank.	I must quickly go to the bank.
Er kann gut Deutsch.	He can speak German well.

The complement verbs (to go, to speak) are implied in the context.

CHAPTER 10

Im Restaurant — *John and Sabine at the restaurant*

- John and Sabine find a nice table in the shade and proceed to order lunch. They are having a really pleasant time.

- All about ordering and paying for meals.
- Introduction to the names of meals and food.
- Useful phrases and vocabulary.

- Word order, subordinate clauses. Conjunctions: 'daß', 'weil', 'wenn'.
- Relative pronouns.

Kellner:	**Grüß Gott! Wollen Sie vielleicht hier Platz nehmen?**
Sabine:	Danke, gern. *(whispering to John)* Kommen Sie schnell! Das ist ein guter Platz im Schatten.
John:	Gute Idee! Es ist heute viel angenehmer im Schatten, weil es so heiß ist.
Kellner:	**Bitte schön, die Speisekarte! Etwas zu trinken?**
John:	**Ein helles Bier für mich und Sie?** *(turning to Sabine)*
Sabine:	**Einen Campari Soda für mich, bitte.**

Exercise:	It is a hot day. Order drinks for yourself and a companion or members of your family. Ask one another what you like to drink in hot or cold weather. (Consult the section on 'Food and Drink' in the appendix, p.152-157)

John:	**Was sollen wir bestellen?** Ich verstehe diese Speisekarte gar nicht gut. *(He is peering at the menu, confused by the Austrian names for dishes.)*
Sabine:	Vielleicht kann ich Ihnen helfen, damit Sie besser wählen können. **Man ißt oft Suppe als Vorspeise, danach folgt die Hauptmahlzeit. Als Dessert oder Nachspeise ißt man oft Kompott oder Mehlspeise.**
Kellner:	*(approaching with pad and pencil)* **Möchten Sie bestellen?**

Sabine:	Ich glaube, daß ein Gulasch heute für mich genug ist. *(turning to John)* Versuchen Sie ein Wiener Schnitzel, die Lieblingsspeise hier.
John:	Wenn Sie Wiener Schnitzel empfehlen, dann will ich es gern versuchen.
Kellner:	**Einmal Gulasch mit Kartoffeln, einmal Wiener Schnitzel mit gemischtem Salat.**
Sabine:	Als Dessert, Früchtebecher mit Eis und Sahne, für Sie auch? *(John nods in agreement)*
Kellner:	**Zweimal Früchtebecher mit Eis und Sahne.**
John:	*(having enjoyed his meal and the company even more)* Das beste Mittagessen meines Lebens! *(indicates his intention to pay)* **Herr Ober, zahlen bitte!**
Kellner:	**Zusammen oder getrennt?**
John:	**Alles zusammen.** *(ignoring Sabine's protests)*
Kellner:	**Bitte schön, die Rechnung.**
John:	375S *(puts down 400S)*. **Das stimmt so, danke schön.**
Kellner:	Danke vielmals, auf Wiedersehen.

For further information look up 'Food and Drink' (p.152-157).

der Kellner	waiter	**die Hauptmahlzeit(en)**	main dish, main meal
der Schatten	shade	**die Suppe(n)**	soup
dunkles Bier	dark beer	**das Gulasch**	beef stew with paprika
helles Bier	light beer		
		die Lieblingsspeise	favourite dish
das Gericht(e)	dish	**das Wiener Schnitzel**	veal or pork escalope in breadcrumbs
die Speise(n)	dish		
die Vorspeise(n)	starter	**die Mehlspeise(n)**	dessert made with flour (strudels, pastry dishes)
das Dessert(s)	dessert		
die Kartoffel(n)	potato	**die Nachspeise(n)**	dessert
der Salat(e)	(side) salad	**der Nachtisch(e)**	dessert
gemischt	mixed, meaning different types of salad		

das Kompott(e)	stewed fruit	**der Früchtebecher**	fruit-cup
der Obers	cream (Austria)	**das Eis**	ice-cream
		die Sahne	cream
zahlen	to pay		
der Ober	(head) waiter		
die Rechnung	bill	**einmal/zweimal**	once/twice
		" "	one(two) portion(s)
die Mehrwertsteuer	V.A.T.		
die Bedienung	service charge	**das stimmt so**	that is okay

(Tips of between 5% and 10% are about right in addition to V.A.T. and service charge.)

folgen	to follow	**schnell**	quickly
versuchen	to try	**gar nicht**	not at all
		als	as
		danach	after that

empfehlen	to recommend
bestellen	to order
wählen	to choose

Was empfehlen Sie?	What do you recommend?
Was möchten Sie bestellen?	What would you like to order?
Was möchtest Du?	What would you like?
Ich möchte .../wir möchten ...	I would like .../we would like ...
Haben Sie ...?	Have you ...?

		***damit**	so that
Ich bin Vegetarier.	I am a vegetarian.	***daß**	that
Ich bin Diabetiker.	I am a diabetic	***weil**	because
Ich bin allergisch auf ...	I am allergic to ...	***wenn**	if
		* see p.95	

kein Fleisch, kein Alkohol	no meat, alcohol,
kein Fett, keine Butter	no fat, butter
keine Sahne, Milch	no cream, milk
keine Nüsse etc.	no nuts etc.

Noch etwas?	Anything else?
Noch eine Flasche Wein.	Another bottle of wine.

Danke vielmals, herzlichen Dank, schönen Dank, vielen Dank, danke schön.
These are all terms used to say **'thank you'** politely.

Exercises:

Eating out (Make good use of the reference section 'Food and Drink' p.152-157)

1. **You are entertaining a business contact** in a very exclusive restaurant. Money is no object. Find out what your guest would like to eat. Make your choice, then discuss what you would both like to drink. Ask the waiter if he could recommend a good wine.

2. **A family with two children are having a meal.** One child is quite small and does not like fish. Another child, a teenager, is a vegetarian. Discuss their choice of food and drinks.You are taking the part of a parent and/or the children.

3. **Two students are having a budget meal.** Put yourself in their shoes and work out an appropriate dialogue.

Work in pairs. Jot down a few relevant sentences and use them as a basis for your conversation. Communication is all here. Again, grammar mistakes are bound to creep in, not to worry, your tutor will be able to correct them when necessary.

Subordinating conjunctions and subordinate word order

When sentences are introduced by (* p.94):

'damit' (so that), **'daß'** (that), **'weil'** (because), **'wenn'** (if, whenever) **and some other conjunctions to be mentioned later, the word order changes.**

The main verb goes to the end of the sentence.
(see examples below)

main clause	subordinate clause
Wir wollen hier sitzen,	**damit** wir im Schatten **sind.**
Vielleicht wissen Sie,	**daß** unsere Kinder Vegetarier **sind.**
Ich möchte ein Eis,	**weil** es viel zu heiß für eine Suppe **ist.**
Ich fahre nach Berlin,	**wenn** ich wieder Urlaub **habe.**

Grammar terminology (subordinate clauses, conjunctions etc.) goes back to the times when all this referred to Latin which has quite a few grammar and structure similarities with German. As I don't want to deprive established and budding grammarians of an explanation, I'll now try to clarify matters a bit more, attempting to be as succinct as possible.

Subordinating conjunctions e.g. as, because, if, that etc. (see box, p.95) are words which connect sentences and make them into so-called subordinate (dependent) clauses because they become dependent upon the main clause and could not stand on their own (see the previous examples of main and subordinate clauses at the bottom of p.95). That is why we refer to subordinating conjunctions, subordinate clauses and in German to subordinate word order.

Exercises:

There are four examples of subordinate word order in the previous dialogue, p.92-93. Can you find them?

Write them down and note the position of the verb.

Correct the following subordinate clauses:

1. Es ist gut, daß wir haben genug Wein.
2. Geh schnell, damit du kommst nicht zu spät.
3. Er hat keine Zeit, weil er muß gehen.
4. Wunderbar, daß Sie kommen zu unserer Party.
5. Hier ist Kleingeld, damit du kannst telefonieren.

Now form three short sentences using some of the conjunctions you have met.

The relative pronouns 'der', 'die', 'das' and **'welcher', 'welche', 'welches'** both meaning **'who'** or **'which', also start subordinate clauses and send the verb to the end.**

Wir essen einen Fisch, **der (welcher)** aus der Donau **kommt**.
Das ist eine Flasche Wein, **die (welche)** nicht kalt genug **ist**.
Das ist ein Ei, **das (welches)** zu hart **ist.**

The relative pronouns above take similar case endings to the definite article (see Grammar Survey, p.197).

CHAPTER 11

Johns charmante Stadtführerin *John's charming city guide*

- Sabine, a student at Vienna university, decides exam pressure can be forgotten for the afternoon and agrees to be John's tourist guide.
  John promises to show her London at some future time.

- Education, training and qualifications. Jobs and job-titles.
- More subordinate word-order, 'seit' construction.

- At the Post Office.

- **Ein schöner Nachmittag** A pleasant afternoon

A sunny afternoon in Vienna and the start of a friendship.

John: Ein wunderbarer Nachmittag! Haben Sie noch ein bißchen Zeit?

Sabine: Eigentlich muß ich zur Universitätsbibliothek, um für eine wichtige Prüfung zu studieren.

Aber Sie haben recht, heute ist es viel zu schön für die Bibliothek.

John: Fantastisch, für mich ist heute der schönste Tag des Sommers!

Sabine: *(teasing)* Wieso? Der Sommer ist ja noch nicht vorbei, es ist erst Ende Juni.

John: Aber es freut mich, daß Sie noch nicht weggehen.

Sabine: Also für heute will ich Ihre Fremdenführerin sein, statt zu studieren.

John: Was studieren Sie denn?

Sabine: Sprachen, Englisch und Französisch, seit drei Jahren.

John: Meine Universitätszeit liegt schon lange hinter mir. Studieren Sie gern?

Sabine: Doch, das Studium macht mir Spaß, obwohl es nicht immer leicht ist.

John: Sprachen sind sehr wichtig, denn man braucht sie heutzutage in fast allen Berufen.

Nochmals vielen Dank für Ihre Hilfe, zuerst im Restaurant und jetzt als meine charmante Fremdenführerin.

Sabine: **Nichts zu danken,** vielleicht brauche auch ich einen Fremdenführer, wenn ich nach London komme.

John: **Das tue ich sehr gern,** denn in London gibt es sehr viele Sehenswürdigkeiten.

der Nachmittag(e)	afternoon	**studieren**	study
die Prüfung(en)	exam	**liegen**	to lie
die Universität(en)	university	**rechthaben(s.)**	to be right
		weggehen(s.)	to leave
die Bibliothek(en)	library		
das Studium(dien)	course, studies		
es freut mich	I am pleased	**es macht Spaß**	to enjoy
die Sprache(n)	language		
die Fremdsprachen	foreign languages		
der Beruf(e)	job, profession		
		nochmals	yet again
das Ende	end	**vorbei**	past
der Juni	June	**noch nicht**	not yet
der Tag	day	**erst**	only (re. time)
die Hilfe(n)	help	**leicht**	easy
		wichtig	important
der Fremdenführer(-)	tourist guide (m.)	**fantastisch**	fantastic
die Fremdenführerin(nen)	tourist guide (f.)	**charmant**	charming
heutzutage	nowadays	**fast**	almost
Wie so?	How come?	**obwohl**	although

um ...... zu ... in order to ....
Ich fahre mit dem Taxi, **um** schnell nach Hause **zu** kommen.

seit (+Dative) **since**
seit drei Jahren for three years

The present tense is used instead of the perfect, as in English:
Seit wann **lernen Sie** Deutsch? Since when **have you been learning** German

More about Subordinate Word Order:

'obwohl' (although) also sends the verb to the end of a sentence, it too introduces dependent clauses like **'wenn','weil', 'daß', 'damit'** (see: Chapter 10, p.95)

Exercises:

Try to find examples of subordinate clauses in the previous dialogue. Write them down and note the position of the verb.

Answer the following questions:

Warum sind Sprachen sehr wichtig?	Weil ....
Warum ist der Sommer noch nicht vorbei?	Weil ....
Wann braucht Sabine John als Fremdenführer?	Wenn ....
Warum studiert Sabine heute nicht?	Weil ....
Warum freut sich John?	Weil ....

verb, verb construction

... subordinate clause ...**verb, verb** ... main clause ...

1st element verb (gehe): 2nd element

Wenn ich nach London **komme, gehe** ich zu Madame Tussauds. (*)

subordinate clause main clause

(Notice the position of 'gehe'!)

Wenn ich nach London **komme, will** ich zu Madame Tussauds gehen.

subordinate clause main clause

('will' is the main verb here)

(*) In the main clause the verb is always the second element. Here it is preceded by a subordinate clause which is the first element, therefore the verb ('gehe') follows. A complete summary of all the relevant aspects relating to German word order can be found on p.198-199 in the appendix.

Translate:

Although languages are interesting, they are not always easy.
If you visit London, summer is always a good time.
Although I am studying now, I am working in the evening.

Education and Qualifications

Germans, Austrians and Swiss people are very aware of the importance of qualifications as determining factors for success in their working lives. Their education system is very structured with important exams at various stages. Career prospects depend on gaining the relevant certificate for one's chosen vocation or profession. There is very little leeway or allowing for compensating factors if the required certificates have not been gained.

der Schulabschluß (das Schulabschlußzeugnis)	school leaving certificate
der Hochschulabschluß Diplom, Magister, Doktorat)	successful completion of a university course

die mittlere Reife	A very useful certificate taken at 16 years of age preparing students for a vocational career-path.
das Abitur	university entrance qualification gained after finishing 'Gymnasium' (similar to a high school or grammar school)
die Matura	the equivalent to 'Abitur' in Austria and Switzerland

die Schule	school	**das Gymnasium**	grammar school
die Grundschule	primary school	**die Hochschule**	university
die Hauptschule	secondary school	**die Universität**	university
die Realschule	intermediate school	**die Berufsschule**	technical college
die Abendschule	night school		

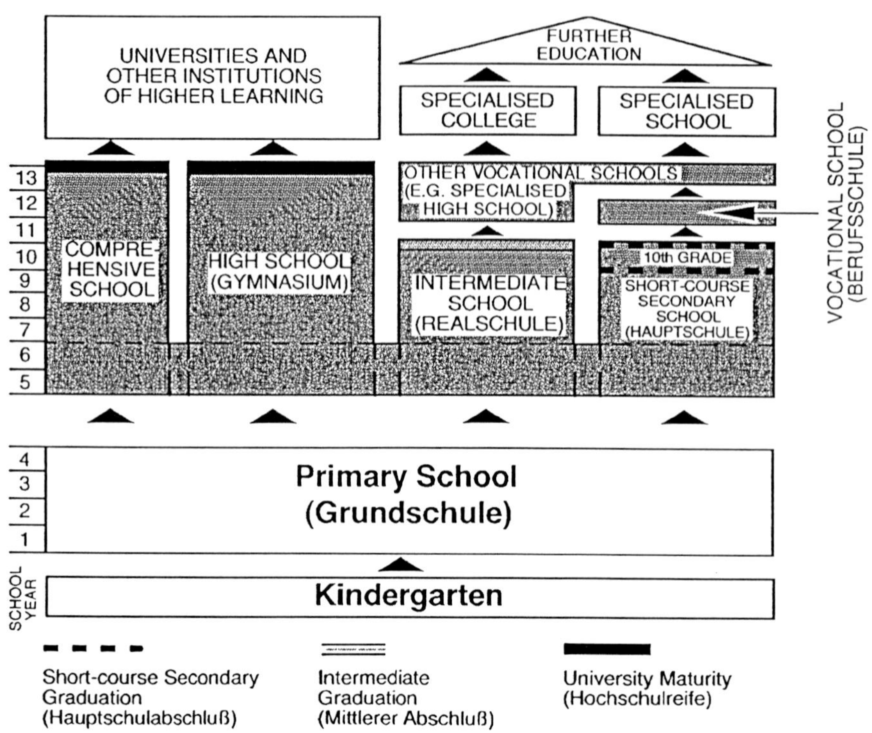

- **Work** die Arbeit (see p.168-169, 'Job titles')

der Arbeiter(-)	worker
der Facharbeiter(-)	skilled worker
der Angestellte(n)	salaried employee
der Beamte(n)	salaried employee in public service, civil servant (very favourable conditions of service)

der Handwerker(-)	someone working in a craft or trade
der Lehrling(e)	apprentice
der Meister(-)	fully qualified 'master' of his craft or trade (only after taking a 'Meister-prüfung', the qualifying exam, can you set up in business as e.g. a tailor, plumber or hair dresser, etc.)
der Selbständige(n)	someone who is self-employed
der Freiberufler(-)	freelance ....

- **WAS SIND SIE VON BERUF?** What is your job, profession?

ich bin Arbeiter, Angestellter, Beamter, ... Germans would often use these terms (an 'r' is added to the masculine form of 'Angestellte', 'Beamte' when no definite article is present)

In Britain it would be appropriate to say:

ich arbeite für die Firma Elektrona	I work for the Elektrona Company
ich arbeite bei (+ name of firm etc.)	I work at (+ name of firm etc.)
ich habe eine Ausbildung als Computerprogrammierer (**die Ausbildung** - training)	I am a trained computer programmer
ich bin Fachmann für ...	I am an expert in ...
ich bin staatlich geprüfte Krankenschwester (der Staat - state, die Prüfung - exam)	I am a qualifed nurse
ich habe e.g. Psychologie **studiert**	I studied psychology
selbständig	self-employed
arbeitslos	unemployed
im Ruhestand	retired
Ich war ...	I was a ...

Exercises:

Study the information above and look at 'Job Titles', p.168-169 in the appendix.

Was sind Sie von Beruf?
Wo arbeiten Sie?
Finden Sie Ihren Beruf (Ihre Arbeit) interessant?
Warum? Warum nicht?
Welche Berufe finden Sie interessant? Warum?
Welche Berufe finden Sie langweilig? Warum?

- **Auf der Post** — At the post office

John: **Wo ist hier ein Postamt**?

Sabine: Ganz **in der Nähe**, hier sind wir schon.

John: **Ich muß einen Brief aufgeben**, auch **ein paar Postkarten**.

Sabine: *(looking at the stamps on the cards)* Die Postkarten sind richtig frankiert, der Brief ist aber schwer!

John: Ich weiß, da sind Fotos drin, ich brauche noch mehr Marken.

(inside the post office)

Sabine: **Hier ist der Schalter für Briefmarken und Postwertzeichen.**

John: **Welche Marken brauche ich für diesen Brief nach England**?

Beamter: Das normale Porto ist ....S. *(weighing the letter)*, dieser Brief ist schwerer, also brauchen Sie noch **Marken im Wert von ....S.**

Sabine: **Wollen Sie den Brief einschreiben lassen**?

John: Gute Idee! Die schönen Photos sollen sicher ankommen.

Beamter: **Eingeschrieben. Bitte füllen Sie diesen Beleg aus**.

John: *(filling out the form)* **Adresse des Empfängers, Unterschrift, Datum**, so, bitte schön (handing the form in to be stamped).

Beamter: **Das macht** ....S, *(taking the money)* stimmt, danke schön, Auf Wiedersehen.

John: **Wo ist denn der Briefkasten?**

Sabine: Draußen rechts von der Eingangstür.

die Post	post, post office	**postlagernd**	post restante
das Postamt(¨er)	post office		
der Schalter(-)	counter	**einen Brief schreiben**	to write a letter
der Brief(e)	letter	**einen Brief aufgeben**	to post a letter
die Postkarte(n)	post card	**einschreiben**	to register
		eingeschrieben	registered
die Marke(n)	stamp		
(das Postwertzeichen)			
das Porto(s)	postage	**lassen**	to have some-thing done
im Wert	to the value of	**frankieren**	to put on stamps
der Beleg(e)	receipt	**ausfüllen**	to fill out
die Adresse(n)	address		
der Empfänger(-)	addressee		
das Datum (Daten)	date		
der Briefkasten(¨)	letter box		
das Paket(e)	packet	**leicht**	light
das Päckchen	small packet	**schwer**	heavy
die Luftpost	air mail		
das Postfach(¨er)	post box		
das Postfach(¨er)	post box		
per Luftpost	by air-mail		
das Gewicht	weight		
die Eingangstür	entrance	**drin (darin)**	in it
		draußen	outside

Exercise:

It is Christmas:
You are arriving at the post office laden with parcels and letters.

Send three different items (letters, cards, parcels, packets) to various places.
Enquire about cost, delivery times, discuss the weight of items to be sent etc.

Write out a dialogue between the post office clerk and yourself.

If in a group, take turns at taking the part of the customer and/or the clerk.

CHAPTER 12

Ein schöner Nachmittag *A beautiful afternoon*

- Getting to know 'Apfelstrudel' and 'Eiskaffee' in a Viennese café.
- Talking about places to go to in the evening. Reserving tickets etc.
- Conversation about newspapers and interests in general.

- The future tense and forms of 'werden', 'würden'.

- **Ein heißer Nachmittag** A hot afternoon

John:	Ein Stadtrundgang macht müde! Darf ich Sie auf eine Erfrischung einladen? Einen Tee oder Kaffee vielleicht?
Sabine:	Danke, da sage ich nicht nein. Diese Hitze heute! Es gibt hier im Burggarten ein hübsches, schattiges Café.
John:	Hier sind wir schon.Wir werden uns da drüben in die Ecke setzen, da ist es schattig.
Sabine:	Ich werde mir einen Eiskaffee bestellen.
John:	Einen Eiskaffee? Den werde ich auch probieren. Wo ist denn die Kellnerin? *(indicating to the waitress)* Fräulein, bitte!
Sabine:	Sie wird gleich kommen. Da ist sie schon.
John:	Zweimal Eiskaffee, bitte.
Kellnerin:	Ein Stück Kuchen oder Torte dazu?
Sabine:	Kennen Sie Wiener Apfelstrudel, John?
John:	Nein, aber ich würde gern ein Stück versuchen, essen Sie auch einen? *(Sabine nods)* Zwei Stück Apfelstrudel, bitte.
Kellnerin:	Mit Schlagobers?
John:	Sabine?
Sabine:	Nein, danke, im Eiskaffee ist ohnedies Schlagobers.

- 'Apfelstrudel' a very nice dessert made of a sheet of very thin filo pastry (roughly 500mm square, made of durum wheat and pulled until 'see through'), brushed with butter and covered in a layer of thinly sliced apple, sprinkled with sugar, cinnamon, sultanas or raisins and breadcrumbs. After that the filo sheet is rolled up, put on a buttered flat roasting dish and baked on a medium heat.

der Stadtrundgang(¨e)	a walk round the city	**sich setzen (r.)**	to sit down
die Erfrischung(en)	refreshment		
die Hitze	heat		
der Burggarten(¨)	park in Vienna		

das Stück(e)	piece	**probieren**	to try
der Kuchen(-)	cake	**versuchen**	" "
die Torte(n)	gateau	**würden**	would
der Apfelstrudel(-)	apple strudel	**werden (+inf.)**	shall, will
der Schlagobers(-)	whipped cream	**werden**	to become

ohnedies	in any case	**schattig**	shady
		(sonnig	sunny)

'Fräulein' is used when summoning a waitress (whether she is a 'Miss' or not)

'werden' (shall, will) not to be confused with **'würden'** (would)

ich werde	**wir werden**	**ich würde**	**wir würden**
du wirst	**ihr werdet**	**du würdest**	**ihr würdet**
Sie werden	**Sie werden**	**Sie würden**	**Sie würden**
er		**er**	
sie wird	**sie werden**	**sie würde**	**sie würden**
es		**es**	

Future Tense

forms of werden (see above) + infinitive

ich werde kommen	I shall/will come I shall be/will be coming
ich werde am Montag kommen	note the position of the infinitive (kommen), more about word order in the appendix, p193.

Exercises:

There are a few examples of the future in the previous dialogue. Can you find them?

Translate:
I shall go to Germany soon.
Will you drive or fly?
We shall visit you soon.
When will you be visiting us?
He/she will be coming tomorrow.
What time will they arrive?

- **werden** on its own means **'to become' or 'going to be'**

Ich werde müde.	I am becoming tired.
Er wird Pianist.	He is becoming/going to be a pianist.

Answer:

Was wird ein Medizinstudent? (See: 'Job titles' on p.168-169, appendix)
Was werden Babys?
Was wird ein Junge/Mädchen?
Wie wird das Wetter morgen?
Wie werden die Temperaturen? (das Grad(e) - degree)

- **'würden'** - would be

Ich würde gern kommen.	I should/would like to come.
Würden Sie mich bitte anrufen?	Would you please give me a call?

Answer: Was würden Sie jetzt gern tun?

- **The article 'der', 'die', 'das' can be used on its own meaning 'this one' or'that one' when referring to a previous noun.**

Der Eiskaffee ..., **der** ist gut.
den trinke ich gern.

- **Was kann man abends tun?** What can one do in the evening?

John: *(later)* Da drüben sehe ich eine Telefonzelle, ich muß schnell meinen Chef, Herrn Müller, im Hotel anrufen.

Sabine: Was wird Ihr Chef heute abend unternehmen?

John: Er wird sicher mit seiner Frau ausgehen. Ins Theater oder in die Oper.

Sabine: Werden Sie mitgehen?

John: Ich würde das gern tun. Leider ist mein Deutsch nicht gut genug für das Theater und für die Oper bin ich nicht musikalisch genug.

Sabine: Aber es gibt ja eine Menge anderer Veranstaltungen und Aufführungen:

Operetten, Musicals, Jazz- und Popkonzerte. Es gibt auch jede Menge Kinos, Diskos und Tanzlokale sowie Restaurants und Heurige, wo man einen schönen Abend verbringen kann.

Kaufen wir doch eine Zeitung, da können wir uns gleich informieren, was es gibt.

die Telefonzelle(n)	phone box	**unternehmen**	to do, undertake
		mitgehen	to accompany
das Theater(-)	theatre		
die Oper(n)	opera	**verbringen**	to spend
		informieren (r.)	to inform oneself
die Veranstaltung(en)	event		
die Aufführung(en)	performance	**Was gibt es?**	What is on?
die Vorstellung(en)	performance	**da drüben**	over there
die Operette(n)	operetta		
das Musical(s)	musical	**musikalisch**	musical
das Konzert(e)	concert	**eine Menge**	a lot of
		jede Menge	any number of
das Kino(s)	cinema		
die Disko(s)	discos		
das Tanzlokal(e)	dance establishment		
der Heurige(n)	originally farmhouses surrounded by vineyards, serving their own wine and food. Nowadays very popular taverns.		
das Gasthaus(¨er)	pub, inn - where food and drink are always available till late at night. Often shut on Mondays ('Ruhetag' rest-day)		
das Wirtshaus(¨er)	same as above: pub, inn		

- **Entertainment** additional vocabulary

der Klub(s)	club	**das Parkett**	stalls
der Verein(e)	association, club	**I Rang**	dress circle
der Sportverein(e)	sports club	**II Rang**	upper circle
		III Rang	gallery
der Empfang(¨e)	reception	**die Mitte**	centre
		die Seite	side
die Zusammenkunft(¨e)	get-together		
die Versammlung(en)	meeting, gathering		
die Ausstellung(en)	exhibition	**der Vortrag(¨e)**	lecture
die Vorführung(en)	presentation	**die Lesung(en)**	reading

- **Entertainment:** **Booking tickets, seat reservations**

Haben Sie Karten für ...?	Have you any tickets for ...?
Bitte reservieren Sie zwei Karten unter dem Namen ...	Please reserve two tickets in the name of ...
Wann müssen wir die Karten abholen?	When do we have to collect the tickets?
Eine Stunde vor der Vorstellung.	One hour before the performance starts.
Was kosten die Karten?	How much are the tickets?

- **Entertainment:** **Key Phrases:**

Was kann man abends unternehmen?	What can one do in the evenings?
Was gibt es?	What is on?
Was werden wir heute abend machen?	What shall we do this evening?
Was meinst Du? (Was meinen Sie?)	What do you think?
Wohin sollen wir gehen?	Where shall we go (to)?
Kannst Du (können Sie) etwas vorschlagen?	Can you suggest something? (vorschlagen - to suggest)

Willst Du einen	**Spaziergang**	**machen?**	Do you want to go for a walk?
Wollen Sie einen	**Stadtbummel**	**machen?**	" " round town?
	einen Rundgang	"	" " on a tour?

• **Entertainment:**	**Key Phrases ctd.:**
Man kann ins Kino, Theater, etc. gehen.	One can go to the cinema, theatre etc.
Man kann auch ...	One can also ...
Wir gehen oft ...	We often go ...
Es gibt ...	There are ...
Wann beginnt ... ?	When does ... start?
Wie lange dauert ...?	How long does ... take?
Wann ist ... zu Ende?	When does ... end?

Exercises:

1. **Team or pair work. Work out a dialogue between two people wanting to spend a pleasant evening. Act it out in class.**

   a. Two people on a business trip wanting a relaxing evening.
   b. A young couple on honeymoon.
   c. A retired couple, very culturally minded.

2. **How do you (your family, friends) like to spend special occasions?** Answer in German having jotted down some ideas.

- **Am Zeitungskiosk** At the newspaper kiosk

John: *(After his pleasant walk round town with Sabine, John is keen to buy a British newspaper, almost at any cost it seems.)*

Welche englische Zeitung haben Sie?

Man: **Fast alle englischen und amerikanischen Tageszeitungen, auch die meisten Zeitschriften.**

(John buys a paper but is shocked to find the price about five times more than he is used to paying.)

John: Der Preis ist ja enorm!

Sabine: Klar, die Zeitung kommt täglich mit dem Flugzeug, deshalb ist sie teuer. Hier ist eine Wiener Zeitung.
(handing the money to the newspaper seller)

John: Nichts gegen österreichische Zeitungen. Für mich sind aber **Nachrichten und Berichte** aus Großbritannien, Amerika und Übersee sehr wichtig, da unsere Firma weltweite Handelsbeziehungen hat.

Sabine: Für Sie ist **Information über Politik, Wirtschaft und Finanz** natürlich sehr relevant. Ich interessiere mich sehr für Artikel über **Wissenschaft und Kultur.**

John: Viele Zeitungen sind voller Artikel über Skandale, Morde und Verbrechen.

Wichtigere aktuelle Themen sind die Umwelt, die dritte Welt, Arbeitslosigkeit, Atomenergie, Abrüstung, Krieg und Frieden, das Flüchtlingsproblem u.s.w.

Finden Sie das nicht auch?

Sabine: Ja, natürlich! (somewhat absent minded, looking at the events page)
Wunderbar, heute abend ist viel los!

die Tageszeitung(en)	daily paper	**enorm**	enormous
die Zeitung(en)	paper	**klar**	obviously
die Zeitschrift(en)	magazine	**täglich**	daily
die Nachricht(en)	news		
der Bericht(e)	report	**Wiener**	Viennese
der Artikel(-)	article	**(die) Übersee**	overseas

die Handelsbeziehung(en)	trade relations	**die Politik**	politics
der Handel(-)	trade	**die Wirtschaft**	economy
die Beziehung(en)	relationship, connection	**die Finanz(en)**	finance
die Wissenschaft(en)	science	**der Mord(e)**	murder
die Kultur(en)	culture	**der Skandal(e)**	scandal
		das Verbrechen(-)	crime
das Thema(en)	subject, theme		
die Umwelt	environment	**die Atomenergie**	atomic energy
die dritte Welt	the third world	**die Abrüstung**	disarmament
die Arbeitslosigkeit	unemployment		
der Krieg(e)	war	**der Frieden(-)**	peace
das Flüchtlingsproblem	the refugee problem		
weltweit	world wide	**nichts gegen**	nothing against
relevant	relevant	**da**	as, because
voller	full of	**aktuell**	current

sich interessieren für ... to be interested in ...

Exercises:

Sie lesen oft Zeitungen und Zeitschriften, für welche Themen interessieren Sie sich, Ihre Familienmitglieder, Freunde und Bekannten?

Ich interessiere mich für ...
Mein Mann (Freund, Bruder, Vater, Sohn) interessiert sich für ...
Meine Frau (Freundin, Schwester, Mutter, Tochter) interessiert sich für...
Wir interessieren uns für ...
Meine Kollegen interessieren sich für ...
Meine/unsere Hobbies sind ...

(See also 'Leisure' on p.164 in the appendix)

Some additional vocabulary:

die Musik	music	**die Technik**	technology
die Malerei	painting	**der Computer**	computer
die Kunst(¨e)	art	(der Rechner	")
das Theater(-)	theatre	**die Geschichte**	history
die Oper(n)	opera	**der Sport**	sport

No article is used **when making general statements.**

Ich interessiere mich für Berichte oder Artikel über Musik.

(You would not say: .... über **die** Musik.)

Das Zeitgeschehen und aktuelle Themen current affairs

Germans, Austrians and Swiss people take a lively interest in current affairs and like to comment on it. They are well informed and are not worried about passing an opinion. They will also be interested in your opinion. However, unless you feel very confident about your language skills and background knowledge, it is wise to avoid potentially sensitive subjects.

Newspaper kiosks and tobacconists do not only sell papers and magazines (p.110)

die Tageszeitung(en)	daily paper
die Zeitung(en)	paper
die Zeitschrift(en)	magazine

They also sell stamps and tickets for public transport. These can be purchased in advance and in bulk. Tickets bought singly on trams, buses and underground trains, work out much more expensive.

die Fahrkarte(n)	ticket
die Vorverkaufskarte(n)	a ticket bought in advance
die Marke(n)	stamp

CHAPTER 13

Eine Verabredung für den Abend *A date for the evening*

- John asks Sabine continue as his tourist guide.
- Perfect tense with 'haben'. Formation of past participles.
- Word order.

John: Ich habe gerade mit meinen Freunden telefoniert. Sie haben mich gefragt, wo ich den ganzen Nachmittag war. Sie haben auf mich gewartet.

Sabine: Was haben Sie geantwortet, daß Sie einen Stadtrundgang gemacht haben?

John: Ich habe auch gesagt, ich habe eine sehr nette Fremdenführerin gefunden. Die habe ich zum Mittagessen und später zu Kaffee und Kuchen eingeladen.

Meine Freunde haben gelacht und gefragt: "Haben Sie sich auch für den Abend verabredet?"

Sabine: Und ...?

John: Ich habe nicht verneint. Jetzt hoffe ich sehr, daß Sie nichts für heute abend vorhaben.

Sabine: Eigentlich muß ich für meine Prüfung studieren, aber ich werde eben morgen sehr konzentriert arbeiten. Ich kann Sie doch nicht allein abends in einer fremden Stadt herumlaufen lassen.

John: Das ist großartig, daß die Wiener Mädchen so nett zu ihren Touristen sind. Kein Wunder, daß Wien eine populäre Stadt ist!

der Stadtrundgang	a walk round town	**eben**	just
verabreden (r.)	to arrange to meet		
antworten	to answer	**fragen**	to ask
etwas vorhaben	to plan to do something	**verneinen**	to say 'no'
herumlaufen (s.)	to run around, to walk about	**hoffen**	to hope
großartig	great, wonderful		

PERFECT TENSE (I)

(formed with 'haben' and past participle)

When talking about the past, the perfect tense is often used not just for talking about events that have just happened (as is the case in English) but also about what happened a long time ago.

A German speaker would quite happily say: "Ich habe vor 30 Jahren in Berlin gelebt und habe dort mein Deutsch gelernt." This tense can therefore be used in the narrative sense whenever you want to talk about the past. It adds a note of liveliness to your account.

Perfect Tense (I)

The perfect tense formed by the forms of the auxiliary verb 'haben' and the past participle of a verb.

regular verbs
e.g.lachen (to laugh)

	auxilliary	past participle
ich	**habe**	**gelacht**
du	**hast**	**gelacht**
Sie	**haben**	**gelacht**
er sie es	**hat**	**gelacht**

etc.
(forms of 'haben', p.)

I have laughed, I laughed

irregular verbs
e.g.finden

	auxilliary	past participle
ich	**habe**	**gefunden**
du	**hast**	**gefunden**

etc.

Stem vowels often change in this group, one of the reasons why they are called 'irregular' ('strong') verbs.

More information about this group of verbs in Chapter 15.

I have found, I found

Some regular past participles:		Some irregular past participles:	
telefoniert*	(telefonieren)	begonnen	(beginnen)
studiert	(studieren)	gesehen	(sehen)
gefragt	(fragen)	gekommen	(kommen)
gesagt	(sagen)	gefunden	(finden)
gelacht	(lachen)	getrunken	(trinken)
geantwortet**	(antworten)	gegessen	(essen)
gewartet**	(warten)		
gemacht	(machen)		
verabredet***	(verabreden)		
verneint***	(verneinen)		

(See: List of Irregular Verbs, p.200)

* verbs ending in -'ieren' do not have a 'ge'- prefix.
** when the verb stem ends in 't' an 'e' is inserted before the ending 't'.
*** verbs starting with unstressed syllables like 'ver'-, 'ent'-, 'be'-, 'emp'-, 'zer'-, 'er'-, 'ge'-, do not prefix with 'ge'- on the past participle.

Word Order

main clause

Ich **habe** ein gutes Hotel **gefunden**. — Past participle at the end.

subordinate clause

.........., **weil** ich ein gutes Hotel **gefunden habe**. — Auxiliary at the end.
.........., **daß** er das Buch **mitgebracht hat**. — In separable verbs the 'ge' goes between prefix and verb.

(see also **Word Order** in the appendix, p.198-199)

Perfect (I) practice

1. Study the forms of 'haben' (p.114), then write them down from memory.

2. Look through the previous dialogue and find examples of the perfect tense.

3. Turn to p.115, look at the way past participles of regular verbs are formed, study the footnotes and write down the past participles of:

machen e.g. gemacht	wohnen
lernen	besuchen
meinen	bestellen
leben	arbeiten
rasieren	interessieren

4. Let's try to find some more past participles. This time we will pick ten common verbs from the list of irregular verbs in the appendix, p.200.

5. Translate into English:

Hast Du lange gewartet?
Wir haben das immer gesagt.
Was haben Sie mich gefragt?
Alle haben über den Film gelacht.
Für wann haben wir uns verabredet?

4. Now answer a few questions:

Wo haben Sie als Kind gelebt?
Wo haben Sie später gewohnt?
Welche Schulen haben Sie besucht?
Wo haben Sie bis jetzt gearbeitet?
Was haben Sie letztes Mal im Restaurant bestellt?
(letztes Mal last time)

- **In der Apotheke** At the chemist

Hay fever strikes. John's medication is only available on prescription. Oh dear, he will have to see a doctor! Sabine's company is greatly appreciated.

John: *(sneezing repeatedly)* Entschuldigung! *(sneeze)* Entschuldigung! *(sneeze)* Entsch.........hatschu!!!

Sabine: **Gesundheit! Was ist denn los?**

John: Zu dumm! **Mein Heuschnupfen hat begonnen,** viel zu früh!

Sabine: Haben Sie ein Medikament dagegen?

John: Nein, leider nicht hier.

Sabine: **Eine Apotheke!** Kommen Sie, hier bekommen Sie sicher einen Nasenspray oder Tabletten.

Chemist: Bitte schön?

John: Ich habe starken Heuschnupfen. In England nehme ich 'Nosene', **hätten Sie diese Tabletten vielleicht?**

Chemist: **Diese Tabletten sind rezeptpflichtig, haben Sie ein Rezept?**

John: Leider nicht.

Chemist: **Nebenan ist ein praktischer Arzt, er hat jeden Nachmittag Ordination.** Er wird das Medikament sicher gleich verschreiben.

John: Gut, dann gehen wir gleich dorthin. Sabine, kommen Sie mit?

Sabine: Natürlich, Sie armer Patient brauchen Hilfe.

die Apotheke(n)	dispensing chemist's shop only		
die Drogerie(n)	For medication over the counter, toiletries, films, etc.		
die Ordination(en)	surgery		
der praktische Arzt	general practitioner	**rezeptpflichtig**	available on prescription only
das Rezept(e)	prescription		
der Apotheker(-)	chemist	**verschreiben**	to prescribe
der Arzt(¨e)	doctor	**mitkommen (s.)**	to come, go with someone
das Medikament(e)	medication		

der Heuschnupfen(-)	hay fever		
der Spray(s)	spray		
die Tablette(n)	tablet	**Gesundheit!**	Bless you!
der Patient(en)	patient	(die Gesundheit	health)
die Nase(n)	nose		
Hätten Sie ...?	Would you have ...?	Hätten Sie Tabletten gegen ... ?	
		zu früh	too early
Zu dumm!	How annoying!	**arm**	poor
		dagegen	against that
		nebenan	next door

- **Beim Arzt** At the doctors

John just wants his prescription for hay fever, but this doctor is thorough!

Secretary: **Guten Tag, haben Sie einen Termin?**

John: Leider nicht, **ich habe plötzlich Heuschnupfen bekommen** *(sneeze)* und ...

Sabine: John hat sein englisches Medikament nicht mit, vielleicht kann der Herr Doktor...

Secretary: Er kann sicher helfen. Nehmen Sie Platz, Sie werden nicht lang warten müssen.

(a little later)

Doctor: Sie haben eine Pollenallergie?

John: Ja, das heiße Wetter, die vielen Blumen ...

Doctor: Sie wollen, daß ich 'Nosene' verschreibe? Das ist ein relativ starkes Mittel.

John: Aber es hilft mir sofort.

Doctor: Es wirkt schnell, das stimmt. Aber es hat manchmal unangenehme Nebenwirkungen. Ich möchte Sie zur Sicherheit kurz untersuchen.

John: *(horrified)* Aber ich bin ja ganz gesund!

Doctor: Macht nichts, machen sie nur den Oberkörper frei, ich will Sie nur abhören.

John: *(relieved, not a full examination, thank God!)*

Doctor: *(listening to John's chest)* Alles ist in Ordnung, keine Bronchitis, kein Katarrh.

Hier ist Ihr Rezept. Nehmen Sie nicht mehr als drei Tabletten pro Tag.

der Arzt(¨e)	doctor	**wirken**	to work
die Ärztin(nen)	lady doctor	**untersuchen**	to examine
der Termin(e)	appointment	**freimachen**	to bare,
der Pollen(-)	pollen		to uncover
die Allergie(n)	allergy	**abhören**	to sound
das Mittel(-)	remedy		one's chest
		unangenehm	unpleasant
die Nebenwirkung(en)	side effects	**gesund**	healthy
der Oberkörper	chest, torso		
die Bronchitis	bronchitis		
der Katarrh	catarrh		
zur Sicherheit(en)	to be sure	**beim (bei dem)**	with or at the ...
		nicht mehr als	not more than

The doctor	**'der Arzt'**	is addressed as	**'Herr Doktor'**
	'die Ärztin'		**'Frau Doktor'**

Many professional people are also addressed in this way having gained a high academic qualification (das Doktorat) in their specific field.

The nurse **'die Krankenschwester'** is addressed as **'Schwester'**.

Practically everybody is a member of a health insurance, **'die Krankenkasse'**, which issues the patient with forms called **'der Krankenschein'**. One of these is handed to the doctor every time a patient goes to see him. The doctor fills in the form stating the nature of the complaint, treatment, etc., and passes the form on to the local office of the 'Krankenkasse' which pays him according to a nationally agreed scale. Additional benefits can be gained from private health insurance or simply paying more in special circumstances.

In general it is worth noting that doctors and hospitals will not as yet attempt to rid themselves of the patient at the first possible moment in the interests of efficiency. You will find them thorough, attentive, even fussy in an effort to look after you.

• **Wie fühlen Sie sich?**	How do you feel?
Ich fühle mich ganz /nicht gut **Mir ist schlecht**	I am feeling not/quite well I am feeling unwell/sick
Ich habe Schmerzen in ... **Mein Knie tut weh.**	I have a pain in ... My knee hurts.
Muß ich ins Spital (Krankenhaus)? **Im Krankenwagen?**	Do I have to go to hospital? In the ambulance?
Ich kann nicht ... **atmen, schlafen, essen, gehen, stehen ...**	I cannot ... breathe, sleep, eat, walk, stand ...
Brauche ich ein Röntgen?	Do I need an X-ray?
Was kostet die Behandlung? **Wie lange dauert die Behandlung?**	How much is the treatment? For how long will I need treatment?
Was soll ich tun? **Was muß ich machen?**	What should I do? What must I do?

Exercise : (pair work)

Look at the phrases above and the information provided in the appendix:
Work out a dialogue pretending you need the doctor for something.

This exercise usually creates a lot of hilarity in a class or group and provides a bit of fun after struggling with difficult terminology.

If you are working on your own do the exercise all the same - try not to get depressed!

There is light on the horizon, the story is gaining in interest.

As you are no longer new to the language you should be able to cope with a bit more continuous text and find reading new material quite rewarding.

The following chapters are designed to provide students with some pleasant reading practice, while continuing to learn more about grammar, e.g. past tenses and how to use them, new structures and other aspects of learning German.

CHAPTER 14

John fährt mit der Straßenbahn. *John takes the tram*

- He wants to get ready for his evening date with Sabine.
- Travelling by public transport
- The Imperfect. Word order.
- Dative verbs and constructions, 'mögen'.

Am späten Nachmittag sagte John 'Auf Wiedersehen' zu Sabine. Er ging zur nächsten Haltestelle und wartete auf eine Straßenbahn. Sie kam schnell, er mußte nicht lange warten.

In der Straßenbahn waren viele Touristen, viele wußten nicht, wo man Fahrkarten bekommt. Man sollte sie schon vor dem Einsteigen kaufen, denn alle Züge sind heutzutage schaffnerlos.

John kaufte seinen Kartenblock an einem Kiosk bei der Haltestelle. Er konnte einem älteren Amerikaner helfen, der brauchte nämlich eine Karte, also verkaufte John ihm eine.

Er kam nach kurzer Fahrt im Hotel an und traf dort seine Bekannten wieder. Diese saßen im Hotelfoyer und warteten auf ein Taxi. Sie fragten John, wohin er abends gehen wollte. John wußte es noch nicht genau.

Er sagte: 'Ich treffe mich um 8 Uhr mit Sabine, sie weiß bestimmt, wo wir einen schönen Abend verbringen können'.

'Dann wünschen wir einen schönen Abend und viel Vergnügen', sagten seine Freunde.

Sabine fuhr inzwischen mit der Untergrundbahn nach Hause in ihre Wohnung. Dort zog sie sich schnell um.

John wusch und rasierte sich und machte sich sorgfältig fertig. Auch er wollte gut aussehen, denn er war von Sabine sehr beeindruckt.

Das merkten seine Freunde natürlich und neckten ihn deshalb ein bißchen. Darüber lachten sie alle, mit einem Wort die Stimmung war richtig gut. Herr und Frau Müller freuten sich auf ihren Abend in der Wiener Oper und John auf sein Rendezvous mit Sabine.

die Haltestelle(n)	stop	**einsteigen in+acc.(s.)**	to get into
die Untergrundbahn(en)	underground train	**aussteigen aus+dat.(s.)**	to get out of
der Kartenblock(s)	a block of tickets		

der/die Bekannte(n)	friend, acquaintance	**verbringen**	to spend
		wünschen	to wish
das Wort(e)	word	**sich fertig machen**	to get ready
das Foyer(s)	foyer, lobby		
die Stimmung(en)	mood	**schaffnerlos**	without conductor
das Rendezvous(-)	date		
Viel Vergnügen!	Have a good time!		
am späten Nachmittag	late in the afternoon	**richtig**	really
		bestimmt	definitely
abends	in the evening		
nächst	next	**bei**	near by, at
		wohin	where (to)
heutzutage	nowadays	**zurück**	back
nämlich	namely, actually	**älter**	older, elderly
genau	exactly	**beeindruckt**	impressed

The verbs on the left are listed in the order in which they occur in the text to help you with the translation.

Imperfect	Infinitive
sagte (said)	sagen (to say)
ging (went)	gehen* (to go)
wartete (waited)	warten (to wait)
kam (came)	kommen* (to come)
mußte (had to)	müssen* (must)
waren (were)	sein* (to be)
wußten (knew, pl.)	wissen* (to know)
kaufte (bought)	kaufen (to buy)
konnte (could)	können* (can)
brauchte (needed)	brauchen (to need)
traf (met)	treffen* (r.) (to meet)
fragten (asked, pl.)	fragen (to ask)
saßen (sat, pl.)	sitzen* (to sit)
fuhr (travelled)	fahren* (to travel)
zog sich um (changed)	umziehen* (r.) (to change)
machte (made)	machen (to make, do)
wusch (washed)	waschen* (r.) (to wash)
rasierte (shaved)	rasieren (r.) (to shave)
wollte (wanted)	wollen* (to want)
merkten (noticed)	merken (to notice)
neckten (teased)	necken (to tease)
lachten (laughed)	lachen (to laugh)
freuten (looked forward)	freuen (r.) (to look forward)

* irregular verb

The majority of verbs are regular (sometimes called 'weak').
In your list of irregular verbs, p.200, you will be able to check whether a verb is regular or not. The third column shows the imperfect form.

From experience I know that by now some students are going to turn their eyes to heaven and start sighing. Are you aware though that we have the same division in English? You have regular verbs like 'to live' with a past tense form of 'lived' adding an -'ed' ending. Those make up the majority of English verbs. But look at e.g. 'to find' or 'to bring', you don't say, 'he finded' or 'he bringed' but 'he found' and 'he brought'. These are irregular verbs which change their stem vowels and take different endings.

The imperfect or simple past tense ('simple' because there is no auxiliary like e.g. 'haben' present) is used in the narrative sense to talk about past events, just like the perfect.

How to form the Imperfect Tense:

regular verbs*		**irregular verbs****	
lachen - to laugh		**kommen** - to come	
ich lach**te**	(I laughed)	ich kam	(I came)
du lach**test**	etc.	du kam**st**	etc.
Sie lach**ten**		Sie kam**en**	
er		er	
sie lach**te**		sie kam	
es		es	
wir lach**ten**		wir kam**en**	
ihr lach**tet**		ihr kam**t**	
Sie lach**ten**		Sie kam**en**	
sie lach**ten**		sie kam**en**	

* An 'e' is inserted if the stem ends in 'd' or 't': warten - wart**ete**
** These verbs very often show a **stem vowel change** as is also the case in English. ('find' but in the imperfect or past tense 'found')

When **writing** about the past however, the imperfect is used in reports, formal accounts etc. Here the perfect would seem a little too lively, almost colloquial.

The name 'imperfect' does not imply an incomplete action as is the case in other languages.

Irregular verbs are listed separately in the appendix, p.200.
Try to remember the forms of the more commonly used ones (below).

finden	**fand**
sitzen	**saß**
beginnen	**begann**
trinken	**trank**
kommen	**kam**
gehen	**ging**
fahren	**fuhr**
stehen	**stand**
sprechen	**sprach**
bin (sein)	**war**
haben	**hatte**

Modal verbs: their endings follow the regular pattern

können	**konnte** (could)
müssen	**mußte** (had to)
sollen	**sollte** (should)
mögen	**mochte** (liked)
wollte	**wollte** (wanted)

Some do, however, change their stem vowels.

Word Order

The same principles apply as in the present tense.

Er **ging** in sein Büro.	Verb - second idea.
Gestern **ging** er in sein Büro.	Inversion as the verb needs to be the second element.
Er **ging** gestern abend **aus**.	Separable verb - prefix at end of sentence.
Weil er gestern abend **ausging**.	Subordinate clause - prefix does not separate.

Translate into German:

1. We spoke German, she found her book, he went to Berlin, they began to eat, you had to go, we wanted to see, she could not come, I was there.

2. What did people do?
Describe a part of the centre of the picture of a German town (p.38)
Pretend everything happened a while ago.

3. Describe part of the picture showing a German/Austrian/Swiss landscape, p.50. Pretend everything happened a while ago.

4. What did you do yesterday? Just a few sentences, using the imperfect tense.

- **In der Straßenbahn** On the tram

Close encounters with a ticket inspector.

Inspector: Ihre Fahrkarte bitte!

Tourist: *(embarrassed looking)* Ich ..., ich habe keine. Hier ist kein Schaffner. Wo kann man Karten kaufen?

Inspector: *(pointing at a sign)* Unsere Züge sind schaffnerlos, Sie bekommen Karten an Kartenschaltern, Automaten und Kiosks.

Tourist: *(flustered)* Entschuldigung, das wußte ich nicht.

Inspector: Am besten steigen Sie bei der nächsten Haltestelle aus. Dort bekommen Sie Vorverkaufsfahrscheine in einem Kiosk.

Tourist: *(relieved)* Vielen Dank!

Inspector: Fahrkarten bitte! *(frowning while examining John's ticket)* Diese Karte ist nicht entwertet.

John: *(bemused)* Wo kann man das tun?

Inspector: *(pointing)* Hier ist die Maschine dafür, sie müssen die Karte in den Schlitz stecken.

John: Ach, Entschuldigung, das habe ich nicht gewußt. Muß ich jetzt Strafe zahlen?

Inspector: Eigentlich schon...., sind Sie zum erstenmal in Wien?

John: *(nodding eagerly)* Ja, und die Wiener sind alle sehr nett!

Inspector: Finden Sie? Also, für heute haben Sie Glück, ich bin auch ein netter Wiener. Sie brauchen keine Strafe zahlen. Aber halten Sie nächstesmal eine gültige Karte bereit!

der Schaffner(-)	conductor	**schaffnerlos**	without conductor
der Fahrschein(e)	ticket	**entwertet**	cancelled
der Schlitz(e)	slot	**gültig**	valid
der Vorverkaufsfahrschein(e) (**der Vorverkaufsschein**)	ticket bought in advance	**stecken**	to push into
Strafe zahlen	to pay a fine		
nächstesmal	next time	**Glück haben**	to be lucky
zum erstenmal	for the first time	**bereit halten**	to have ready

Although the previous dialogue ends on a happy note, this is very often not the case. Inspectors travel in twos, dressed like ordinary people and frequently board trams and underground trains to check on tickets. Make sure you have a valid ticket, cancelled at the start of your journey.

It is much cheaper to buy tickets in bulk (they are issued in pads or as tickets for several trips) at kiosks, underground stations or ticket machines. Fines for not being able to produce a valid ticket are quite high.

- **Verbs followed by the Dative** (ctd. from Chapter 9)

e.g. **sagen** (to say) **Was sagen Sie mir?** What are you saying to me?

No 'zu' is required , just the dative form of the following noun or pronoun.

sagen	(to say)	**danken**	(to thank)
erzählen	(to tell)	**geben**	(to give)
berichten	(to report)	**helfen**	(to help)
antworten	(to answer)	**folgen**	(to follow)
schreiben	(to write)	**erlauben**	(to allow)
senden	(to send)	**gestatten**	(to permit)
schicken	(to send)	**dienen**	(to serve)

- **Dative constructions with:**

gefallen	(to like, see p.163)
schmecken	(to taste, like the taste of)
gehören	(to belong)
gelingen	(to succeed)

Die Rose gefällt mir.	I like the rose.
Mir gefällt die Rose.	" " "
Mir gefallen die Rosen.	I like the roses.
Die Rosen gefallen mir.*	" " "
Wie schmeckt es Dir/Ihnen?	How do you like it? (in relation to food and drink)
Wie schmeckt Ihnen der Wein?	How do you like the wine?
Schmecken Ihnen deutsche Weine?*	Do you like German wines?
Das Buch gehört mir.	The book belongs to me.
Die Bücher gehören ihm.*	The books belong to him.
Dir gelingt es sicher.	You will definitely succeed.

(* Don't forget plural verb endings when plural nouns are present.)

As a general expression of liking the modal verb 'mögen' (irregular, see list) **can also be used:** Ich mag Sport. Mögen Sie klassische Musik? Du magst Fisch nicht.

Some more familiar dative constructions

• **Wie geht es Dir/Ihnen?**	How are you?
• **Mir geht es gut. Es geht mir gut.**	I am well.
• **Mir ist kalt/warm/heiß.**	I am cold/warm/hot.
• **Ist Dir/Ihnen kalt/warm/heiß?**	" " "
• **Es macht (mir) nichts.**	It does not matter. (to me)
• **Es ist mir gleich (egal).**	It is all the same to me.

Exercises:

Dative Verbs and Pronouns

Translate:

1. I say to him ...
2. He tells her ...
3. They write to us ...
4. She answers you ...
   (all forms)
5. We help them ...
6. They thank us ...
7. You follow me ...

Dative constructions

Translate:

1. I like the house. (gefallen)
2. We like the parks. (gefallen)
3. He likes beer. (schmecken)
4. She likes wine. (schmecken)
5. The Mercedes belongs to me. (gehören)
6. We/they succeed ... (Es gelingt ... ... zu ...)

CHAPTER 15

Eine große Enttäuschung *A big disappointment*

- It is 8 o'clock on a warm summer evening. John has been waiting for well over an hour to meet Sabine, as arranged earlier in the afternoon. Why has she not arrived yet?

- How to return tickets, cancel arrangements, change bookings and ask for a refund on damaged or faulty goods.

- Pluperfect tense, more imperfect. Three ways of expressing 'when'.
- Relative pronouns.

Sabine und John hatten sich um 8 Uhr vor dem Stephansdom in Zentrum Wiens verabredet. John war schon seit viertel vor acht da, hatte sich auf eine Bank gesetzt und wartete.

Er hatte nachmittag eine englische Zeitung gekauft und begann zu lesen, allerdings konnte er sich nicht gut konzentrieren.

Die Zeit verging und Sabine war immer noch nicht da. Es war schon viertel nach acht, dann halb neun, jetzt wurde John langsam traurig. Wo war Sabine? War sie vielleicht krank? Ein Unfall?

Er hatte nicht einmal eine Telephonnummer oder Adresse. Endlich hatte er ein ideales Mädchen gefunden, hübsch, klug, sehr nett und völlig natürlich. Hatte er sie vielleicht verloren?

Er beobachtete die Leute, die vorbeigingen; viele Touristen, auch Einheimische, junge Leute, die Arm in Arm vorbeispazierten. Nur Sabine war nirgends zu sehen.

Als er eine weitere Viertelstunde bis viertel vor neun gewartet hatte, gab er die Hoffnung auf, sie je wiederzusehen.

die Enttäuschung(en)	disappointment	Telling the time, p.147	
die Viertelstunde(n)	quarter of an hour		
die Bank (¨e)	bench	**viertel vor acht**	quarter to eight
der Unfall(¨e)	accident	**viertel nach acht**	quarter past eight
		halb neun	half past eight
der Einheimische(n)	native	**viertel vor neun**	quarter to nine

der Arm(e)	arm	**lesen**	to read
die Hoffnung	hope	**vergehen**	to pass
		hatte	had
allerdings	however	**beobachten**	to watch
immer noch nicht	still not ...	**verlieren**	to lose
nicht einmal	not even	**vorbeigehen (s.)**	to walk past
		vorbeispazieren (s.)	to saunter past
krank	ill	**aufgeben (s.)**	to give up
traurig	sad	**wiedersehen (s.)**	to meet again
klug	clever		
weiter	further	**je**	ever
		als	when (in the past)

PLUPERFECT TENSE (I)

This tense is formed by combining the forms of 'hatten' with a past participle.

ich	**hatte** gekauft (I had bought)	wir	**hatten** gefunden
du	**hattest** gesagt	ihr	**hattet** gemacht
Sie	**hatten** gefragt	Sie	**hatten** telefoniert
er sie es	**hatte** begonnen	sie	**hatten** getrunken

Word Order

John hatte eine englische Zeitung **gekauft**.	(statement)
Er hatte ein ideales Mädchen **gefunden**.	(statement)
Hatte er sie vielleicht **verloren**?	(question)
Ich hatte mich mit .... **verabredet.**	(reflexive)
Er hatte sich auf eine Bank **gesetzt**.	(reflexive)
weil er sich auf eine Bank **gesetzt hatte**	(sub. clause)

Exercises:

1. We had waited for five minutes.
2. They had read the newspaper.
3. She had found her purse.
4. Had we said that?
5. Had he begun to eat?

Can you form a few sentences using the pluperfect?

'wurde'	imperfect of	'werden'
ich **wurde** du **wurdest** Sie **wurden** er sie **wurde** es	(I became ...)	wir **wurden** ihr **wurdet** Sie **wurden** sie **wurden**

Es wurde sehr kalt.	It became very cold.
Er wurde Arzt, Priester etc.	He became a doctor, priest etc.
Was wurde aus ...?	What became of ...?

Relative pronouns

der, die, das or **welcher, welche, welches** **who, which**

These replace nouns with the same functions, and therefore require the use of cases.

Der Sänger, **der (welcher)** in der Oper singt, ist gut.	Der Sänger, **von dem (welchem)** wir viel hören, ist gut.
Der Park, **der (welcher)** im Zentrum liegt, ist groß.	Der Park, **in dem (welchem)** wir sitzen, ist groß.

In the previous examples you may again have become aware of word order. Sentences introduced by relative pronouns i.e. relative clauses follow the pattern of all other subordinate or dependent clauses. Word Order: see appendix, p.199.

Well, it is not all theory! The German in the next couple of pages will equip you to cope with situations where one often has to steel oneself to cope, even in one's native tongue. Again, you will learn relevant phrases and core vocabulary to help you, if you find yourself confronted with one of the following situations.

- **Wir geben unsere Karten zurück** — We are returning our tickets

John: Guten Abend: *(surprised to see Herr and Frau Müller walking towards him)* **Ist es nicht schon Zeit für die Oper?**

Herr Müller: Die hat schon begonnen aber es ist nicht dieselbe, für die wir Karten haben.

John: **Wieso, was ist denn los?**

Herr Müller: Unser Lieblingssänger in der Hauptrolle ist leider krank.

John: **Werden Sie Ihre Karten zurückgeben?**

Herr Müller: Selbstverständlich, die waren ja enorm teuer. **Wir bekommen den vollen Preis zurück.**

John: Gut, dann ist nichts verloren.

der Lieblingssänger	favourite singer	**zurückgeben (s.)**	to return, give back
die Hauptrolle(n)	leading rôle	**selbstverständlich**	of course
		voll	full

Karten zurückgeben	to return tickets
den Preis zurückbekommen	to get one's money back

- **Herr Müller muß einen Termin absagen** — Herr Müller cancels an appointment

Herr Müller: *(later at the hotel reception)* **Entschuldigen Sie, ich möchte mein Büro in Frankfurt faxen, geht das?**

Receptionist: Ja, natürlich .... Bitte kommen Sie, **die Faxmaschine ist im Büro.**

Herr Müller: Hier ist mein Text:

Kann meinen Termin mit Mr. Jones nicht einhalten. Können Sie absagen? Stornieren Sie bitte den Flug nach London. Wir müssen umbuchen. Vielleicht sind Flugkarten nach New York für nächsten Freitag erhältlich.

Müller

der Text(e)	text
Geht das?	Is it possible?
einen Termin einhalten	to keep an appointment
absagen (s.)	to cancel (dates, appointments)
stornieren	to cancel (tickets, holidays, flights etc.)
buchen	to book
umbuchen (s.)	to change a booking
erhältlich	available

- **Eine Beschwerde** A complaint

Receptionist: **Dieses Fax ist für Sie**, Herr Müller!

Herr Müller: Danke schön, (sighing). Was ist denn jetzt wieder los?

(starts to read)

Eine Beschwerde aus Amsterdam.
Lieferung angekommen, Ware fehlerhaft oder beschädigt.
Der Kunde will reklamieren.
Bevor wir den Preis vergüten, schicken wir Herrn Stoll nach Amsterdam.

Schulz

die Beschwerde(n)	complaint	**sich beschweren**	to complain
die Lieferung(en)	delivery	**ankommen (s.)**	to arrive
		p.p.: angekommen	
die Ware(n)	product, goods		
der Kunde(n)	customer		
		reklamieren	to ask for a refund
		vergüten	to give a refund
fehlerhaft	faulty		
beschädigt	damaged		
das Geld zurückgeben	to give back the money		

Exercises:

How to return tickets, cancelling arrangements, change bookings and ask for a refund on damaged or faulty goods.

1. You have asked the hotel receptionist for tickets to a musical or concert; instead you are given tickets for a show at a nightclub. Complain and insist on your wishes being met.

   e.g. 'Sorry, these are not the right tickets, there must be a mistake or a misunderstanding'. (Da stimmt etwas nicht, das ist ein Mißverständnis.)

2. Make an appointment. Unfortunately you cannot keep it.
   Change the appointment, give a reason, ask for another appointment.
   (ändern - to change)

3. Talk to your travel agent about cancelling a flight and re-booking at a later date. Give a reason, indicate preferences etc.

4. Shopping - you have bought something, e.g. an item of clothing; on closer inspection you find a fault or something you don't like. Explain the nature of your complaint and ask for a refund.

5. Haben Sie einen Lieblingssänger, Lieblingsschauspieler,
   (der/die Schauspieler/in actor)
   oder vielleicht einen Lieblingspolitiker (!) ?

'When' can be expressed in three ways

1.	**When? (in a question)** When are they coming?	**Wann?** Wann kommen sie?
2.	**When ... (in the past)** When he came home.	**Als ...** Als er nach Hause kam.
3.	**When ... (meaning whenever)** He always sings, when he is sitting in the bath.	**Wenn ...** Er singt immer, wenn er im Bad sitzt.

Exercise: Form a sentence for each example of 'when'.

CHAPTER 16

Alles ist wieder gut — *Everything is all right again*

- John and Sabine are reunited at last. Unfortunately their time together is cut short.
- Perfect II (with 'sein'). Pluperfect II (with 'war'). The Passive.
- A car accident and subsequent breakdown on the motorway.

Plötzlich hörte John Sabines Stimme seinen Namen rufen. Er drehte sich schnell um und sah sie auf ihn zulaufen. Ganz außer Atem rannte sie in seine Arme. John hielt sie ganz fest und gab ihr vor Freude einen Kuß. Er war so glücklich! Er hatte nicht umsonst gewartet.

Sabine: Liebling, jetzt hast Du mich geküßt, da darfst Du nicht mehr 'Sie' zu mir sagen.

(Oh dear! Our hero is not really very familiar with 'Du' forms!)

John: Wo bist Du gewesen, ich dachte, es ist etwas passiert.

Sabine: Ich habe solche Angst gehabt, daß Du nicht mehr da bist.
Ich habe mich sehr verspätet, aber das war nicht meine Schuld.
Laß Dir erzählen!

Ich bin um 6 Uhr nach Hause gekommen und bin dann schnell einkaufen gegangen. Als ich nach Hause zurückgekommen bin, habe ich mich fertiggemacht und meine Freundin sagte: 'Komm doch mit, ich will ohnedies in die Stadt fahren'.

Wir sind in ihren alten Volkswagen gestiegen und sie ist in Richtung Stadt gefahren. Aber das Auto ist nicht weit gekommen.
Eine Reifenpanne!

Wir sind ausgestiegen und haben mit dem Radwechsel begonnen. Sehr gut ist das nicht gegangen. Zum Glück ist ein Motorradfahrer vorbeigekommen. Er ist stehengeblieben und hat uns geholfen.

Ich bin die ganze Zeit sehr nervös gewesen, ich habe doch pünktlich kommen wollen. Wir haben natürlich warten müssen, bis unser Helfer in der Not fertig war.

Ich bin so froh, daß Du nicht weggegangen bist!

John: Für Dich, Sabine, warte ich auf immer!

Sabine: Meinst Du das wirklich?

John: Aber natürlich!

der Atem(-)	breath	**hören**	to hear
der Arm(e)	arm	**umdrehen (r., s.)**	to turn round
der Kuß(¨e)	kiss	**rennen**	to run
der Liebling(e)	darling	**laufen**	ditto
		zulaufen..auf (s.)	to run towards
die Angst(¨e)	fear, worry		
Angst haben	to be worried, frightened	**halten**	to hold
		küssen	to kiss
vor Freude	overjoyed	**gewesen** (p.p. of 'sein')	been
nicht meine Schuld	not my fault		
die Reifenpanne(n)	burst tyre	**lassen**	to let
der Radwechsel	wheel swap	**passieren**	to happen
der Fahrer(-)	driver		
das Motorrad(¨er)	motorcycle	**erzählen**	to tell
		verspäten(r.)	to be late
die Welt(en)	world		
		außer	out of
zurückkommen(s.)	to return	**fest**	firm
einsteigen(s.)	to get into ...		
aussteigen(s.)	to get out of ...		
		umsonst	in vain
vorbeikommen(s.)	to come past		
stehenbleiben(s.)	to stop	**zum Glück**	luckily
		Helfer in der Not	helper in distress
auf immer	for ever		
solcher, e, es	such	**nervös**	on edge, nervous
dich (acc. 'du')	you	**pünktlich**	punctually

More imperfect forms in the previous dialogue:

Regular verbs: **hörte** (hören), **drehte sich um** (umdrehen), **sagte** (sagen)

Mixed verbs (regular endings + stem vowel changes): **rannte** (rennen)
dachte (denken)

Irregular verbs: **sah** (sehen), **gab** (geben)

PERFECT TENSE (II)

Verbs of movement or state form the perfect tense with 'sein' instead of 'haben'.

Below is a list of verbs frequently used.

sg.

gehen (go)	**ich bin gegangen**	**I have gone** or I went
laufen (run, walk)	**du bist gelaufen**	**you have run** or you ran
fahren (drive, travel)	**Sie sind gefahren**	**you have driven** or drove
kommen (come)	**er ist gekommen**	**he has come** or came
fallen (fall)	**sie ist gefallen**	**she has fallen** or fell
springen (jump)	**es ist gesprungen**	**it has jumped** or jumped

pl.

fliegen (fly)	**wir sind geflogen**	**we have flown** or flew
bleiben (stay)	**ihr seid geblieben**	**you have stayed** or stayed
werden (become)	**Sie sind geworden**	**you have become** or became
sein (be)	**sie sind gewesen**	**they have been** or were

rennen (run, race)	**ist gerannt**	**has run,** ran
schwimmen (swim)	**ist geschwommen**	**has swum,** swam
wachsen (grow)	**ist gewachsen**	**has grown,** grew
sterben (die)	**ist gestorben**	**has died,** died
passieren (happen)	**ist passiert**	**Wann ist das passiert?**
geschehen (happen)	**ist geschehen**	**Wie ist das geschehen?**
aufstehen (s.) (get up)	**ist aufgestanden**	**has got up,** got up
einsteigen (s.) (get into)	**ist eingestiegen**	**has got into** e.g. a car
aussteigen (s.) (get out)	**ist ausgestiegen**	**has got out** of ditto

PLUPERFECT (II)

The verbs listed in the previous box as well as all other verbs of movement or state combine with **'war'** instead of **'hatte'** to form the pluperfect

sg.

e.g. kommen	ich **war** gekommen	I	**had** come
	du **warst** gekommen	you	**had** come
	Sie **waren** gekommen	you	**had** come
	er	he	
	sie **war** gekommen	she	**had** come
	es	it	

pl.

wir **waren** gekommen	we	**had** come
ihr **wart** gekommen	you	**had** come
Sie **waren** gekommen	you	**had** come
sie **waren** gekommen	they	**had** come

The following separable prefixes are often added to verbs of movement to give directional emphasis:

hin-	away from the speaker	**hinein-, herein-**	into
her-	towards the speaker	**hinaus-, heraus-**	out of, from
weg-	away	**ab-**	off, away
vorbei-	past		

e.g. hinfahren, herkommen, weggehen, vorbeifahren, abfliegen, abfahren

Mein Bruder studiert in Berlin, ich bin **hingefahren**.
Dein Chef ist hier, du bist **hergekommen**.

Der Park war nicht offen, sie ist **weggegangen**.
Ein super Auto ist **vorbeigefahren**.

Concorde ist vor zwei Stunden **abgeflogen**.
Der Intercity ist gerade **abgefahren**.

Perfect Practice

1. Revision:
   Choose one regular and one irregular verb from the verbs listed on p.115, Chapter 13 (Perfect I) and write out all the forms in the perfect tense.

2. Write out the complete perfect forms of: sehen (see list of irreg. verbs, p.200)
   gehen
   fahren

3. Make a few notes and tell us what you have been doing:

	heute	
Was haben Sie	gestern	gemacht?
	am Wochenende	
	letzten Sommer	

   Ask your tutor or consult a dictionary for additional vocabulary if necessary.

4. Scan the text again and tell the story in the present tense.
   (In the 3rd person, e.g. er wartet ..., sie kommt ... etc.)

5. Having looked at the explanations about past tenses try to change your present tense version to one that (has) happened in the past.

Reflexive verbs in the Perfect

some examples:	present	**perfect**
waschen (to wash)	ich wasche mich	**ich habe mich gewaschen**
fertigmachen (to get ready)	du machst dich fertig	**du hast dich fertiggemacht**
duschen (to take a shower)	er duscht sich	**er hat sich geduscht**
rasieren (to shave)	er rasiert sich	**er hat sich rasiert**
anziehen (to get dressed)	sie zieht sich an	**sie hat sich angezogen**
ausziehen (to get undressed)	wir ziehen uns aus	**wir haben uns ausgezogen**
umziehen (to get changed)	Sie (sie) ziehen sich um	**Sie (sie) haben sich umgezogen**
sich erinnern (to remember)	Sie erinnern sich	**Sie haben sich erinnert**
Erinnern Sie sich?	Do you remember?	**Haben Sie sich erinnert?**
Erinnern Sie sich nicht?	Don't you remember?	**Haben Sie sich nicht erinnert?**

Exercise:

Choose two reflexives from the group below and write down all forms in the present and perfect

sich setzen	(to sit down)
sich legen	(to lie down)
sich treffen	(to meet)
sich interessieren	(to be interested)

- **After an exceedingly pleasant evening together, the time has come for John and Sabine to say good-bye.**

John: *(sighing)* Morgen fahren wir wieder zurück nach Frankfurt, es wäre schön, wenn wir noch ein paar Tage in Wien hätten.

Sabine: *(looking at her watch)* Es ist schon spät, John.

John: Dieser Abend soll nie zu Ende gehen.

Sabine: *(whispering)* Ich weiß, aber alles Schöne hat ein Ende.

John: Laß uns nicht vom Ende sprechen, nur von einem neuen Anfang.

Sabine: Du hast recht, die Zukunft beginnt hier!

John: Wir bleiben in Kontakt!

Sabine: Das verspreche ich!

John: Danke für alles, Du warst die beste Fremdenführerin überhaupt.

Sabine: Nichts zu danken! Du warst der netteste Tourist, vergiß Wien nicht!

der Anfang(¨e)	start, beginning	**rechthaben(s.)**	to be right
die Zukunft	future	**bleiben**	to remain, stay
der Kontakt(e)	contact	**versprechen**	to promise
		vergessen	to forget
zu Ende gehen	to come to an end	**überhaupt**	ever, at all

- **Ein Unfall auf der Autobahn** An accident on the motorway

Herr and Frau Müller and John depart early next morning. They hope to arrive in Frankfurt by late afternoon. However, things do not turn out as expected.

Sabine receives a phonecall.

Sabine: Hallo John, wie nett, daß du schon anrufst! Wie geht's?

John: Leider nicht sehr gut.

Sabine: Was ist denn los?

John: **Wir haben einen Unfall gehabt**, einen Zusammenstoß.

Sabine: Um Gottes Willen, **wo ist das passiert**?

John: **Auf der Autobahn in der Nähe von Passau.**

Sabine: **Wie ist es passiert, wer war schuld**?

John: Es hat geregnet und **wir mußten bremsen** - wegen einer Baustelle. **Der Wagen** hinter uns hat die Warnungstafeln übersehen und **konnte nicht mehr halten**. Er krachte hinten in unseren Mercedes hinein.

Sabine: So ein Pech. **Ist jemand verletzt**?

John: **Der Lenker und Beifahrer** des anderen Wagens haben zum Glück nur **leichte Verletzungen**. Uns ist nichts passiert, unser Mercedes ist ja wie ein Panzer.

Sabine: Gott sei Dank, Ihr habt Glück gehabt! **Sind die Autos sehr beschädigt?**

John: **Der Schaden am Mercedes ist geringfügig**, aber das andere Auto ....

Sabine: **Ist es ganz kaputt**?

John: **Totalschaden**. Es war ein Trabant. Er wird gerade abgeschleppt. Unser Mercedes wird in Frankfurt repariert, die Stoßstange wurde eingedrückt.

der Zusammenstoß(¨e)	collision	**schuld sein**	to be at fault
Um Gottes Willen!	Good God!	**regnen**	to rain
die Autobahn(en)	motorway	**bremsen**	to break

die Baustelle(n)	road works, building site	**übersehen**	to overlook
		hineinkrachen (s.)	to smash into
die Warnungstafel(n)	warning sign	**abschleppen (s.)**	to tow away
das Pech(-)	bad luck	**reparieren**	to repair
		eindrücken (s.)	to push in
der Lenker(-)	driver		
der Beifahrer(-)	passenger	**hinter**	behind
die Verletzung(en)	injury	**verletzt**	injured
der Panzer(-)	tank (military)	**geringfügig**	minimal
der Schaden(-)	damage	**beschädigt**	damaged
der Totalschaden(-)	a write off		
die Stoßstange(n)	bumper	**kaputt**	damaged, in need of repair

jemand	somebody, anybody	**zum Glück**	luckily
niemand	nobody		

THE PASSIVE

The Passive Voice (when something is happening to the subject of a sentence) is formed by the tense forms of 'werden' and the past participle.

Der Taxifahrer **wird von John gefragt.** The taxi-driver (subject) **is being asked by John.**

but

John fragt den Taxifahrer. John asks the taxi-driver.

This is called the Active Voice. Here the subject (John) carries out the action.

Present tense	**ich werde gefragt**	I am (being) asked
	es wird gesagt	it is (being) said
	Das Auto wird repariert	the car is being repaired
	Es wird abgeschleppt	it is being towed away
Imperfect	**ich wurde gefragt**	I was (being) asked
Perfect	**ich bin gefragt worden**	I have been asked
Pluperfect	**ich war gefragt worden**	I had been asked
Future	**ich werde gefragt werden**	I shall (will) be asked

Exercises:

Translate into German:

1. He is being asked.
2. We are being asked.
3. They were asked.
4. Were you asked?
5. She has been asked.
6. Has he been asked?
7. They had been asked.
8. Had she been asked?
9. Will you be asked?
10. I will be asked.

The use of 'by' in the passive

'by' meaning 'by means of' is mostly translated by using **'von' (+ Dative),** also occasionally 'durch' (+ Accusative), **not 'bei'** which means 'at' or 'nearby'.

The house is being built **by** a building firm.
Das Haus wird **von** einer Baufirma gebaut.

Die Zeitung wird **von** vielen Leuten gelesen.
The paper is being read **by** many people.

Exercises:

Make passive constructions of the three short sentences below by starting the sentence with the last noun, the object, thus converting it into the subject.

Example: Der Mann sieht den Hund. Der Hund wird von dem Mann gesehen

1. Der Mechaniker hört Popmusik.
2. Ich vergesse das Buch.
3. Sie übersehen die Baustelle.

Try all tenses (see box on previous page).
(Don't forget to check the dative forms of 'ich', and 'Sie', p.186, as they will follow 'von' which requires the dative.)

- **Eine Panne auf der Autobahn** A breakdown on the motorway

Having emerged unscathed from their accident our trio are pleased to be able to resume their journey again. However, the Trabant seems to have had its revenge after all.

Herr Müller: *(at the wheel)* Was ist denn das? So ein Lärm von hinten! Hört ihr das auch?

John: Ja, es ist der Auspuff, glaube ich.

Herr Müller: So können wir nicht weiterfahren. Hier ist ein Telefon (**Notruf** - emergency number), dummerweise müssen wir auf dem Pannenstreifen stehenbleiben.

Man: Hallo, **ADAC Pannendienst!**

Herr Müller: Guten Tag, wir stehen auf der Autobahn in Richtung Straubing hinter der Raststätte Grüntal. **Etwas ist mit dem Auspuff nicht in Ordnung.**

Man: **Welchen Wagen haben Sie?**

Herr Müller: Einen Mercedes, 200E.

Man: **Ich sende gleich einen Streifenwagen**, er kommt in zirka zehn Minuten.

ADAC patrol: *(having looked at the problem)* Der untere Teil des Wagens und der Auspuff sind **beschädigt**. Sie müssen **den Wagen abschleppen** lassen.

Herr Müller: Das kommt mir sehr ungelegen, ich muß dringend morgen früh in Frankfurt sein.

ADAC patrol: In Grüntal ist eine sehr gute **Reparaturwerkstatt**. Dort können Sie auch **ein Auto mieten**.

Herr Müller: *(turning to John)* Dann ist die Sache nicht so schlimm.

die Panne(n)	breakdown	**weiterfahren (s.)**	to drive on
der Auspuff	exhaust	**abschleppen (s.)**	to tow away
der Pannendienst(e)	breakdown service	**stehenbleiben (s.)**	to stop
in Richtung	in the direction of	**mieten**	to rent, hire
die Reparaturwerkstatt(¨en)	repair garage		

die Sache(n)	the matter, thing	**es kommt mir ungelegen**	
die Raststätte(n)	service station	it is inconvenient for me	
der Streifenwagen	patrol car		

der untere Teil	the lower part	**so ein(e)**	such a
dummerweise	regrettably	**von hinten**	from the rear
morgen früh	early tomorrow morning	**schlimm**	bad, serious

Exercise:

Haben Sie schon einmal eine Panne gehabt? Erzählen Sie, was passiert ist.

Perfect practice:

Beschreiben Sie einen Unfall

Some exam papers have questions on accidents to be related in a past tense. If you . should ever have to report a real incident to the police in any of the German speaking countries you might be thankful to have practised with the help of the terminology following.

Imagine you were a witness at the scene of an accident or crime. Can you tell someone about it. Study the terminology and make rough notes, work in pairs or a group.

Terminology: Motor Accidents (p.178-179)

APPENDIX

Comprehensive supplementary reference source, containing a wealth of general back-up information as well as business and technical language. Additional teaching, practice and learning material, which can be drawn on at any stage throughout the course to extend the range of the core language contained in the main text.

• ZAHLEN — NUMBERS

(after 20 the units come first)

1	**eins**	11	**elf**	21	**einundzwanzig**
2	**zwei**	12	**zwölf**	22	**zweiundzwanzig**
3	**drei**	13	**dreizehn**	23	**dreiundzwanzig etc.**
4	**vier**	14	**vierzehn**	30	**dreißig**
5	**fünf**	15	**fünfzehn**	31	**einunddreißig etc.**
				40	**vierzig**
6	**sechs**	16	**sechzehn**	50	**fünfzig**
7	**sieben**	17	**siebzehn**	60	**sechzig**
8	**acht**	18	**achzehn**	70	**siebzig**
9	**neun**	19	**neunzehn**	80	**achtzig**
10	**zehn**	20	**zwanzig**	90	**neunzig**

100	**(ein)hundert**	**1000**	**(ein)tausend**
200	**zweihundert**	**2000**	**zweitausend**
201	**zweihundert(und)eins**	**2350**	**zweitausenddreihundertfünfzig**
	etc.		**etc.**

10 000 zehntausend **1 000 000 eine Million** **1000 000 000 eine Milliarde**

• DIE UHRZEIT — TELLING THE TIME

Wieviel Uhr ist es?	**Wie spät ist es?**	What is the time?
es ist zwei Uhr		it is two o'clock
es ist viertel nach zwei or	**viertel drei**	quarter past two
es ist halb drei (!!!!!!!!)		half past two **NOT** half past three
es ist viertel vor drei or	**dreiviertel drei**	quarter to three
es ist drei Uhr		it is three o'clock

es ist fünfMinuten vor/nach	**viertel drei**	it is five minutes to/past quarter past two
	halb drei	half past two
	dreiviertel drei	quarter to three

die Minute(n)	minute	**nach**	past,after
die Sekunde(n)	second	**vor**	before
		die Uhr geht nach	the clock/watch is slow
die Stunde	hour		
die halbe Stunde(n)	half hour	**die Uhr geht vor**	the clock/watch is fast
die viertel Stunde(n)	quarter of an hour		

There is no a.m or p.m. in German, one just refers to e.g. 8 o'clock in the morning/evening (acht Uhr früh/abend) or 12 o'clock midday/ midnight (zwölf Uhr Mittag/ Mitternacht) using **früh** **Vormittag** **Mittag** **Nachmittag** **Abend** **Nacht** to be specific.

Wie spät ist es jetzt? Wie spät ist es in zwei Stunden? Wie spät ist es in/ war es vor 12 Stunden? Wann gehen Sie zur Arbeit? Wann kommen Sie nach Haus? (um .... Uhr)

• DAS DATUM — THE DATE

Welches Datum ist heute? — What date is it?
Der wievielte ist heute? — ditto

Das Datum ist	**der erste Januar**	the date is	the first of January
	der zweite Februar		the second of February
	der dritte März		the third of March
	der vier**te April**		etc.
	der fünf**te Mai**		
	der sechs**te Juni**		
	der sieb**te** (siebente) **Juli**		
	der ach**te August**		
	der neun**te September**		
	der zehn**te Oktober**		
	der elf**te November**		
	der zwölf**te Dezember**		
after twenty:	der zwanzig**ste**		
	der dreißig**ste**		
	der hundert**ste**		
	der tausend**ste**		

Heute ist der fünf**te** sieb**te** neunzehnhundert und .../ zweitausend und eins:
Today is the 5th July 19..., 2001 etc.
5.7.19../2001etc.

Ich komme am 5.7.19..		I am coming on the....
Ich komme am fünften siebt**en neunzehn ...**		ditto
Ich komme am fünften Juli neunzehn ...		ditto
es ist fünfMinuten vor/nach	**viertel drei**	it is five minutes to/past quarter past two
	halb drei	half past two
	dreiviertel drei	quarter to three

• ZEITANGABEN — EXPRESSIONS OF TIME

der Tag(e)	day	**der Monat(e)**	month
die Woche(n)	week	**vierzehn Tage**	two weeks
zwei Wochen	two weeks	(often used)	

der Montag	Monday	**der Freitag**	Friday
der Dienstag	Tuesday	**der Samstag**	Saturday
der Mittwoch	Wednesday	**(Sonnabend)**	
der Donnerstag	Thursday	**der Sonntag**	Sunday

am Montag, Dienstag etc. on Monday, Tuesday etc.

- **ZEITANGABEN (ctd.)** **EXPRESSIONS OF TIME**

in der Früh	early in the morning	**zu Mittag**	at lunchtime
am Morgen	in the morning	**am Nachmittag**	in the afternoon
am Vormittag	in the late morning	**am Abend**	in the afternoon
in der Nacht	in the night		

heute today	**heute früh**	this morning	(early)
	heute morgen	this morning	(up to about 10 o'clock)
	heute vormittag	this morning	(10 -12 o'clock)
	heute Mittag	today at lunchtime	
	heute Nachmittag	this afternoon	
	heute Abend	this evening/tonight	
	heute Nacht	in the night	

Combinations as above:		**vorgestern**	the day before yesterday
gestern	yesterday	**morgen**	tomorrow
gestern Abend/Nacht	last night	**übermorgen**	the day after tomorrow

in der Früh	early in the morning	**zu Mittag**	at lunch time
am Morgen	in the morning	**am Nachmittag**	in the afternoon
am Vormittag	in the later morning	**am Abend**	in the evening
		in der Nacht	at night

der Feiertag(e)	a day when shops, banks etc. are closed
der Werktag	working day
der Feierabend	the time after one has finished work in the afternoon
der Urlaub(e)	holiday
die Ferien	vacations

- **DIE JAHRESZEITEN** **THE SEASONS**

das Frühjahr spring **der Sommer** summer **der Herbst** autumn **der Winter** winter

nächst--	next
letzt--	last
übernächst--	the one after next
vorletzt--	the one before last

On the next, last etc. day, month...

am nächst**en**/letzt**en**/übernächst**en**/vorletzt**en**	**Tag**
am nächst**en**/letzt**en**/übernächst**en**/vorletzt**en**	**Sonntag, Montag etc.**
im nächst**en**/letzt**en**/übernächst**en**/vorletzt**en**	**Monat**
im nächst**en**/letzt**en**/übernächst**en**/vorletzt**en**	**Mai, Juni etc.**
im nächst**en**/letzt**en**/übernächst**en**/vorletzt**en**	**Frühjahr, Sommer etc.**
but	
in der nächst**en**/letzt**en**/übernächst**en**/vorletzt**en**	**Woche**

• EINKAUFEN — SHOPPING

Clothes

der Anzug(¨e)	suit (men)
das Kostüm(e)	suit (women)
der Mantel	coat
der Wintermantel	winter-coat
die Hose(n)	trousers
die Jeans	jeans
das Sakko	men's jacket
der Pullover(-)	jumper
das Hemd(en)	shirt
der Anorak(s)	anorak
der Schianzug(¨e)	ski suit
die Schihose(n)	ski trousers
der Schal(s)	scarf
der Handschuh(e)	gloves
die Socke(n)	sock
der Strumpf(¨e)	stocking
die Strumpfhose(n)	tights
die Badehose(n)	swimming trunks (men)
der Schuh(e)	shoe

das Kleid(er)	dress
die Kleidung	clothing
die Bekleidung	ditto
der Hut(¨e)	hat
die Kappe(n)	cap
die Mütze(n)	pull-on hat
das Unterhemd(en)	vest
die Unterhose(n)	underpants
die Unterwäsche	underwear
die Krawatte(n)	tie
der Schlips(e)	ditto
das Halstuch(¨er)	neck tie
der Pyjama(s)	pyjamas
das Nachthemd(en)	nightdress/ nightshirt
die Bluse(n)	blouse
das T-Shirt	T-shirt
der Büstenhalter	Guess what?
der Badeanzug(¨e)	swimsuit (ladies)
der Bikini(s)	bikini

• Materials

das Leder	leather
die Baumwolle	cotton
die (Schaf)Wolle	wool
das Leinen(-)	linen
dick/dünn	thick/thin
klein/groß	small/large
mittelgroß	medium size
leicht	light (weight)
schwer	heavy (also difficult)
kalt/warm/heiß	cold/warm/hot
wasserdicht	watertight

der Kunststoff(e)	plastic
die Kunstfaser(n)	artificial fibre
die Mischfaser(n)	mixed fibres
die Seide(-)	silk
kurz/lang	short/long
hell/dunkel	light/dark
weit/eng	wide/narrow
schön	beautiful
hübsch	pretty
häßlich	ugly
nett	nice
farbfest	colourfast

• EINKAUFEN — SHOPPING

das Kaufhaus(¨er)	store	**das Geschäft(e)**	shop
der Supermarkt(¨e)	supermarket	**der Laden(¨)**	shop
die Abteilung(en)	department	**das Einkaufszentrum**	shopping centre

die Rolltreppe(n)	escalator	**der Stock(¨e)**	floor
der Fahrstuhl(¨e)	lift	**der erste/zweite/dritte/ vierte Stock**	
der Aufzug(¨e)	ditto	the first/second/third/fourth floor	

Welche Größe haben Sie?	What is your size?	**Haben Sie etwas Größeres etc.?**	Have you anything larger etc.than this?
Meine Größe ist...	My size is...		
Kann ich das anprobieren?	Can I try it on?	**Ja, ich nehme das.**	Yes, I will take it.
Wo kann ich hier zahlen?	Where can I pay here?	**Nein danke, das ist nicht, was ich suche.**	No thank you, this is not what I am looking for.
An der Kassa.	At the cash desk.		

• FARBEN — COLOURS

rot/blau	red/blue	Welche Farben mögen Sie?
gelb/grün	yellow/green	('mögen' to like)
weiß/grau	white/grey	Haben Sie eine Lieblingsfarbe?
braun/schwarz	brown/black	Welche?
rosa/lila	pink/mauve	Welche Farbe mögen Sie nicht, ja,
violet/orange	purple/orange	hassen Sie? ('hassen' to hate)

einfärbig	self-coloured	**gemustert**	patterned
bunt	multi-coloured	**gestreift**	striped
karriert	checked	**getupft**	dotted

Sizes

Women	10	12	14	16	18	20	22	British
Damen	**36**	**38**	**40**	**42**	**44**	**46**	**48**	**Continental**
Men	36	38	40	42	44	46	48	British
Herrn	**44**	**46**	**48**	**50**	**52**	**54**	**56**	**Continental**

Shoes	41/2	5-51/2	6-61/2	7-71/2	8	8 1/2	9-91/2	10-101/2	British
	37	**38**	**39**	**40**	**41**	**42**	**43**	**44**	**Continental**

• ESSEN und TRINKEN — FOOD and DRINK

• Die Gemüse (Vegetables)

der Spargel	asparagus	**der Pilz(-e)**	mushroom
die Aubergine(n)	aubergine	**die Kräuter(pl)**	herbs
die Bohne(n)	bean	**die Zwiebel(n)**	onion
der Braunkohl	broccoli	**die Erbse(n)**	pea
der Kohl	cabbage	**die Kartoffel(n)**	potato
das Sauerkraut	pickled cabbage	**Salzkartoffeln**	boiled potatoes
die Karotte(n)	carrot	**Pellkartoffeln**	boiled potatoes in skins
der Blumenkohl(e)	cauliflower	**der Karoffelbrei**	mashed potatoes
die Sellerie	celery	**Bratkartoffeln**	roast potatoes
die Zucchetti(pl.)	courgettes	**die Radieschen(pl.)**	radishes
die Salatgurke(n)	cucumber	**der Rotkohl**	red cabbage
die Rübe(n)	turnip	**das Blaukraut**	ditto (Austria)
die Essiggurke(n)	sweet/sour gherkin	**der Spinat**	spinach
die Salzgurke(n)	salty gherkin	**der Rosenkohl**	sprouts
der Knoblauch	garlic	**der Mais**	sweetcorn
die Essiggurke(n)	gherkin	**die Tomate(n)**	tomato
der Kürbis(e)	marrow	**der Kohlrabi(s)**	a type of turnip
der Lauch	leek	**der Kopfsalat(e)**	lettuce

• Das Obst (Fruit)

der Apfel(¨)	apple	**die Aprikose(n)**	apricot
die Banane(n)	banana	**die Brombeere(n)**	blackberry
die Kirsche(n)	cherry	**die Traube(n)**	grapes
die Pampelmuse(n)*	grapefruit	**die Zitrone(n)**	lemon
die Apfelsine(n)*	orange	**der Pfirsich(e)**	peach
die Birne(n)	pear	**die Ananas**	pineapple
die Pflaume(n)	plum	**die Himbeere(n)**	raspberry
der Rhabarber	rhubarb	**rote Johannisbeeren**	redcurrants
die Erdbeere(n)	strawberry	**schwarze Johannisbeeren**	blackcurrants

(* also 'Grapefruit' and 'Orange')

• Getränke (Drinks)

das Mineralwasser	(natural) mineral water	**das Bier(e)**	beer
die Schorle	wine and soda water	**dunkles/helles Beer**	dark/light beer
der Gespritzte	wine and soda water (Austria)		
der Sprudel	carbonated drink		
der Saft(¨e)	juice	**der Wein(e)**	wine
der Fruchtsaft(¨e)	fruit juice	**der Rotwein**	red wine
der Apfelsaft(¨e)	apple juice	**der Weißwein**	white wine
der Himbeersaft(¨e)	raspberry juice		

- **ESSEN und TRINKEN** **FOOD and DRINK**

- **Some Bavarian/Austrian names for food and drink** (Useful in hotels, restaurants, pubs or when staying with hosts from southern Germany or Austria.)

der Erdäpfel(-)	potato	**Palatschinken**	pancakes
die Fisole(n)	bean	**die Zwetschke(n)**	plum
der Paradeiser(-)	tomato	**die Marille(n)**	apricot
der Karfiol(e)	cauliflower	**Faschiertes**	minced meat
die Sprossen	sprouts	**der Rahm**	cream
der Rettich(e)	radish	**der Obers**	cream
		der Schlagobers	whipped cream
die Schwammerln	edible wild mushrooms	**das Knödel(n)**	dumpling
die Semmel(n)	bread roll	**das Kipferl(n)**	croissant

- **Brot** (Bread)

das Brot(e)	bread	**das Brötchen(-)**	bread roll
der Laib(e)	loaf	**das Toastbrot**	sliced white bread
die Bäckerei(n)	bakers shop	**backen**	to bake
ein Stück Brot	a piece of bread	**eine Scheibe Brot**	a slice of bread

Bread comes in many different shapes and sizes. It varies in colour from white **(Weißbrot)**, light brown **(Graubrot)** and brown to almost black **(Pumpernickel)**.

The colour is determined by the amount of rye in the dough which is left to ferment before being baked. Very often different types of seeds are added resulting in a variety of different flavours.

- **Wurst** (Sausage)

die Wurst(¨e)	sausage	**das Würstchen(-)**	smallish, thin sausage for boiling or frying

Bratwurst is fryed or roasted in the oven, often accompanied by 'Sauerkraut'.
Frankfurter style sausages are simmered in boiling water and eaten with **'Senf'** (mustard).

Germans are very proud of their sausages and rightly so since countrywide there are literally hundreds of different varieties, all very tasty and made of good quality meat.

Broadly speaking they fall into two categories. The lighter textured pinkish red ones, mainly made of pork and lightly smoked should be eaten soon after purchase. The darker salami- style sausages are heavily smoked and will last for quite a while. Generations of mountaineers and travellers have been sustained by this type of sausage. They should be sliced thinly and eaten either on dark farmhouse type bread or on crusty white bread or rolls.

- **ESSEN und TRINKEN** — **FOOD and DRINK**

• **das Fleisch**	(Meat)	**die Innereien**	innards
das Lammfleisch	lamb	**die Leber**	liver
das Kalbfleisch	veal	**die Nieren**	kidneys
das Rindfleisch	beef		
das Schweinefleisch	pork		
der Schinken(-)	ham	**das Geflügel**	poultry
• **das Wild**	venison	**das Huhn(¨er)**	chicken
das Reh(e)	deer	**das Hähnchen**	small chicken
der Hase(n)	hare		
der Fasan(e)	pheasant	**der Truthahn**	turkey also 'Putenfleisch'
		die Gans(¨e)	goose
		die Ente(n)	duck
• **der Käse(-)**	cheese		
• **der Fisch**	(Fish)		
der Thunfisch(e)	tuna	**der Aal(e)**	eel
der Kabeljau	cod	**der Hering(e)**	hering
der Heilbutt	halibut	**der Lachs(e)**	salmon
die Scholle(n)	plaice	**der Karpfen**	carp
die Seezunge(n)	sole	**die Forelle**	trout
der Schellfisch	haddock		
der Hummer	lobster	**der Krebs(e)**	crab/crayfish
die Garnelen	prawns	**die Krabben**	shrimps
geräuchert	smoked	**garniert**	garnished
gebraten	roasted or fried	**gebacken**	baked or fried
paniert	in breadcrumbs	**gesotten**	stewed
gekocht	boiled	**gedünstet**	stewed (Austria)
roh	raw	**gemischt**	mixed/blended
ein Stück	a piece	**das Schnitzel**	escalope/slice
eine Scheibe	a slice	**das Geschnetzelte**	casserole
ein Viertel	a quarter	**die Frikasse**	casserole
die Hälfte	half of	**der Eintopf**	hot pot

Beilagen (served with the meat or fish dish, sometimes charged separately)

Kartoffen	potatoes		
die Nudeln(pl.)	pasta, noodles	**das Knödel**	dumpling
der Reis	rice	**der Kloß(¨e)**	dumpling
Pommes frites	chips	**Chips**	crisps

- **ESSEN und TRINKEN** **FOOD and DRINK**

More information to help you cope with mealtimes.
Das essen die Deutschen gern:

Rinderroulade	rolled up slice of beef, often filled with a thin slice of smoked bacon, sliced mushrooms and a slice of German style sweet-sour gherkin. This is stewed gently with some lightly fried onions, the resulting juices being finished off into a nice sauce with the addition of a dash of German mustard.
Wiener Schnitzel	A thin slice of veal or tender pork in a golden breadcrumb crust.
Jägerschnitzel	A slice of meat topped with mushrooms and vegetables in sauce.
Zigeunerschnitzel	A slice of meat topped with fried onions, tomatoes and peppers.
Sahneschnitzel	A slice of meat in cream sauce.
Gulasch	Very tasty meat stew with onions and paprika.
Braten	is the word for a roast e.g. 'Schweinebraten' - roast pork.
Schinken	Ham, very many varieties, all are delicious.
Eisbein	Very popular dish, lightly smoked knuckle of pork.
Sauerkraut	which is not as bad as it sounds. Fermented, thinly sliced white cabbage. In the hands of a good cook it can be really delicious.
Eintopf	Hot-pot. Popular in northern parts of Germany. Varous ingredients, often potatoes, cabbage, smoked sausage or smoked pork.
Salat	Usually means side-salad.
Platte	Platter, e.g. 'Salatplatte', 'Wurstplatte', 'Käseplatte' etc. A dish with a selection of cold sliced meats, sausage, cheeses etc., garnished with salad vegetables
Aufschnitt	Selection of cold sliced meats, sausage, salami of your choice.
Kasseler	smoked pork
Sauerbraten	spiced beef
Bratwurst	crisply fried or oven-roasted sausage
Tafelspitz	A tender cut of beef, boiled. Very popular in Austria.
Spanferkel	spit-roasted suckling pig
Hähnchen	roast/grilled chicken
Wild	venison
Forelle	trout 'Forelle blau': Trout, poached in water and vinegar + onions, bay-leaves and peppercorns. The vinegar turns the fish a delicate blue colour. 'Forelle Müllerin': Trout, fried in butter and parsley.

- **ESSEN und TRINKEN** **FOOD and DRINK**

das Essen(-)	meal, food	**das Menü**	dish of the day
das Getränk(e)	beverage	**das Tagesgedeck**	ditto
		die Speisekarte(n)	menu
das Frühstück	breakfast	**die Getränkekarte(n)**	wine-list
das Mittagessen	lunch (often the main meal)		
das Abendessen	evening meal (frequently buffet style, cold sliced meats, salami, cheese with bread or rolls.)		

helles/dunkles Bier	light-coloured lager type/dark malty beer
ein kleines/großes Bier	a large/small beer
Kaffee und Kuchen	coffee and cake (mid-afternoon) Coffee is almost always wonderfully aromatic, fairly strong and mainly accompanies sweet foods such as cakes and pastries etc.
die Jause(n)	as above in Austria.
die Speise(n)	dish
das Gericht(e)	ditto
die Lieblingsspeise	favourite dish
die Vorspeise(n)	starter, traditionally soup
die Hauptmahlzeit(en)	main meal
die Nachspeise(n)	dessert
der Nachtisch	ditto
der Kuchen(-)	cake
die Torte(n)	gateau **not** tart

- **Cakes, gateaux and pastries** are quite an experience in German speaking countries, so indulge yourself if you get the chance. People enjoy going to cake shops mid-afternoon, meeting up with a friend or just sitting by themselves enjoying their favourite piece of 'Apfelstrudel', 'Kuchen', 'Torte' or ice-cream with a cup or two of exquisite coffee.

- **das KännchenTee/Kaffee** pot of tea/coffee (enough for two cups)
- **Tea** is of that continental rather anaemic, blond, see-through appearance mostly served with a wedge of lemon. In winter rum or brandy is added and very nice it is too with snow outside. For a stronger brew you only need to ask for an extra tea-bag or two and your problem is solved.

Herr Ober/Fräulein, bitte!	Waiter/waitress please!
Wir möchten bestellen!	We would like to order!
Die Rechnung,bitte!	The bill, please!
Zahlen, bitte!	ditto

- **ESSEN und TRINKEN** — **FOOD and DRINK**

Hat's geschmeckt?	Did you like it? ('schmecken' to taste)
Danke, es hat sehr gut geschmeckt.	It was very nice, thank you.

See also: Chapters 9 and 10

- **When shopping for food the following terminology will be useful.**

Weights		**Bags, tins etc.**	
ein Kilo (1000g) Karotten	a kilo of carrotts	**die Tüte(n)**	bag
ein halbes Kilo (500g) ...	half a kilo of ...	**das Säckchen(-)**	small bag
ein viertel Kilo (250g) ...	quarter of a kilo ...		
		die Packung	packet
ein Pfund (500g) ...	a pound of ...	**die Schachtel(n)**	box
ein halbes Pfund (250g) ...	half a pound of ...	**die Dose(n)**	tin, can
100 Gramm	one hundred grams	**die Marke(n)**	brand
		die Sorte(n)	type/range
ein Liter	one litre	**die Art(en)**	sort/type
ein halber Liter	half a litre	**die (Aus)wahl**	choice
ein viertel Liter	quarter of a litre		

kaufen	to buy	**wählen**	to choose	**probieren**	to try
einkaufen	to shop	**aussuchen**	ditto	**einpacken**	to wrap

See also chapters 8 to 10 for additional information.

Deutsche Häuser

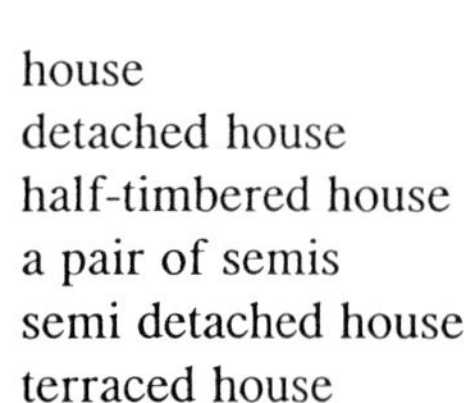

das Haus(¨er)	house
das Einfamilienhaus(¨er)	detached house
das Fachwerkhaus(¨er)	half-timbered house
das Doppelhaus(¨er)	a pair of semis
die Doppelhaushälfte(n)	semi detached house
das Reihenhaus(¨er)	terraced house

die Wohnung(en)	flat
die Mietwohnung(en)	rented flat
die Eigentumswohnung(en)	flat owned by occupier
die Sozialwohnung(en)	municipal, council flat
der Hausherr/die Hausfrau	landlord/landlady
der Vermieter/die Vermieterin	ditto
der Mieter(m.)/die Mieterin(f.)	person renting
der Eigentümer/Besitzer	owner (m.)
die Eigentümerin/Besitzerin	owner (f.)

der Wohnblock(¨e)	block of flats
das Wohnviertel(-)	residential area
die Wohnlage(n)	location

die Villa(en)	large house
der Bungalow(s)	bungalow
der Baugrund(¨e)	building plot

- **DAS HAUS** — **THE HOUSE**

das Zimmer(-) room
das Wohnzimmer(-) living room
das Speisezimmer(-) dining room
das Schlafzimmer(-) bedroom

die Diele(n) hall
das Vorzimmer(-) hall (Austria)

das Fenster(-) window
die Tür(en) door
der Fußboden(¨en) floor
die Kachel(n) tile (Austria)
die Stiege(n) stairs (Austria)
die Toilette(n) toilet

das Möbel(-) furniture

der Tisch(e) table
der Stuhl(¨e) chair
der Sessel(-) chair (Austria)
der (Lehn)sessel easy chair
das Sofa(s) settee
das Buffet(s) sideboard
die Anrichte(n) ditto

der Vorhang(¨e) curtain
die Gardine(n) ditto
der Teppich(e) carpet
die Tapete(n) wallpaper

die Wand(¨e) wall
das Bild(er) picture
das Gemälde(-) painting
das Bücherregal(e) book-shelf
der Kamin(e) fire-place
die Lampe(n) lamp
die Hi-fi Anlage(n) music system
das Radio(s) radio
der Fernseher(-) television set
das Arbeitszimmer study
das Büro(s) office

das WC toilet
das Klo(s) ditto

das Badezimmer(-) bathroom

die Badewanne(n) bath
die Dusche(n) shower
das Waschbecken(-) basin

das Handtuch(¨er) towel
das Badetuch(¨er) bath towel
die Fliese(n) tile
der Wasserhahn(¨e) tap
das Wasser water
die Treppe(n) stairs
die Stufe(n) step

heiß hot **kalt** cold
alt old **neu** new
antik antique
modern modern

groß big **klein** small
mittelgroß medium size

breit wide **schmal** narrow
lang long **kurz** short
hoch high **niedrig** low

sehr very **schön** beautiful
hübsch pretty **häßlich** ugly

oben upstairs
unten downstairs

das Bett(en) bed
das Doppelbett(en) double bed
der Nachttisch(e) bedside table
der Schrank(¨e) cupboard
der Kleiderschrank(¨e) wardrobe
die Kommode(n) chest of drawers

das Federbett(en) duvet
die Decke(n) blanket
das Kopfkissen(-) pillow
die Bettwäsche bedding

• DAS HAUS — THE HOUSE

das Dach(¨er)	roof
der Dachboden(¨en)	loft
der Boden(¨en)	floor
das Dachzimmer(-)	attic
der Ziegel(-)	brick
der Dachziegel(-)	roof tile
die Mauer(n)	wall (outside)
der Flur (die Diele)	hall
der Keller(-)	cellar
der Hobbyraum(¨e)	hobby room
die Garage(n)	garage

• **der Garten(-)**	garden
das Gartenhaus(¨er)	summer house
der Schuppen(-)	shed
der Wintergarten(¨)	conservatory
der Balkon(e)	balcony
die Terrasse(n)	patio

das Erdgeschoß(e)	ground floor
der erste Stock	first floor
der zweite Stock	second floor
der dritte Stock	third floor
der vierte Stock	fourth floor

• **die Küche**	kitchen

der Kühlschrank(¨e)	fridge
der Gefrierschrank(¨e)	freezer
die Waschmaschine(n)	washing machine
der Geschirrspüler(-)	dish washer

der Gasherd(e)	gas cooker
der Elektroherd(e)	electric cooker
die Spüle(n)	sink
der Wasserhahn(¨e)	tap
der Abfluß(¨sse)	drain
das Geschirrtuch(¨er)	tea towel
das Besteck(e)	cutlery
das Messer(-)	knife
die Gabel(n)	fork
der Löffel(-)	spoon
die Küchengeräte	kitchen appliances
die Kaffeemühle(n)	coffee grinder

das Bügeleisen(-)	iron
das Bügelbrett(er)	ironing board
der Kaffeeautomat(en)	coffee machine

der Wandschrank(¨e)	wall cupboard
das Geschirr(e)	dish(es)

die Pfanne(n)	pan
der Topf(¨e)	pot
die Schüssel(n)	bowl
der Krug(¨e)	jug
die Teekanne(n)	tea pot
die Kaffeekanne(n)	coffee pot
die Tasse(n)	cup
die Untertasse(n)	saucer
der Teller(-)	plate
der Wäschekorb(¨e)	washing basket
der Mülleimer(-)	waste bin
der Eimer(-)	bucket
das Tischtuch(¨er)	table cloth
die Serviette(n)	napkin

Exercises: (Das Haus)

If you are still near the beginning of the course (up to chapter 4) try to practise some useful 'Haus' vocabulary by describing the place you live in.
(At this stage it is best to refer to things by means of 'da ist ein, eine'..., 'da sind' ...)

Choose your favourite room and talk/write about it. 'Mein Lieblingszimmer ist...'

When referring to nouns e.g. 'the garden, **it** is big', the gender determines whether **'it'** is referred to as **'er'** (he), **'sie'** (she) or **'es'** (it).

Der Garten	**er** ist groß	(masc.)
Die Garage	**sie** ist lang	(fem.)
Das Haus	**es** ist modern	(neut.)
Die Häuser	**sie** sind modern	(pl.)

For more advanced students (from chapter 5 onwards) 'ich habe ...., wir haben .....,' should also be used. Be aware that this is an opportunity to practise cases.

- **DER GARTEN** — **THE GARDEN**

- **PFLANZEN und BLUMEN** — **PLANTS and FLOWERS**

die Pflanze(n)	plant
der Baum(¨e)	tree
die Blume(n)	flower
der Strauch(¨er)	bush
der Zierstrauch	ornamental bush
die Kräuter	herbs
das Gras(¨er)	grass
die Geranie(n)	geranium
die Rose(n)	rose
die Tulpe(n)	tulip
die Nelke(n)	carnation
das Veilchen(-)	violet
die Narzisse(n)	narcissi
die Osterglocke(n)	daffodil
der Krokus(se)	crocus

der Rasen(-)	lawn
der Teich(e)	pond
das Blumenbeet(e)	flower bed
das Glashaus(¨er)	green house
das Gewächshaus(¨er)	ditto
der Schuppen(-)	shed
die Eiche(n)	oak
die Buche(n)	beech
die Birke(n)	birch
die Weide(n)	willow
die Fichte	spruce
die Tanne	fir
die Föhre(n)	pine
die Kiefer(n)	ditto

Exercises:
Read through the page 'Expressing likes and dislikes', p.163, before answering the questions:
Was sind Ihre Lieblingsblumen? (Which are your favourite flowers?)
Welche Blumen, Bäume und Sträucher haben Sie in Ihrem Garten?
Auf Ihrem Balkon oder Ihrer Terrasse?
(You may have to consult a dictionary for vocabulary not included on this page.)

- **DIE TIERE** **ANIMALS**

der Hund(e)	dog	**der Fuchs(¨e)**	fox
die Katze(n)	cat	**das Reh(e)**	roe deer
das Pferd(e)	horse	**der Hirsch(e)**	stag, red deer
die Kuh(¨e)	cow	**der Hase(n)**	hare
der Stier(e)	bull	**das Kaninchen(-)**	rabbit
das Schwein(e)	pig		
das Schaf(e)	sheep	**das Huhn(¨er)**	chicken
die Ziege(n)	goat	**der Hahn(¨e)**	cockerel
		die Henne(n)	hen
		die Ente(n)	duck
die Schildkröte(n)	tortoise	**die Gans(¨e)**	goose
der Hamster(-)	hamster		
der Goldfisch(e)	gold fish	**die Schlange(n)**	snake
der Papagei(n)	parrot	**der Frosch(¨e)**	frog
der Wellensittich(e)	budgerigar	**die Eidechse(n)**	lizard
		der Krebs(e)	cray fish
die Forelle(n)	trout		
der Karpfen(-)	carp	**der Vogel(¨)**	bird
		die Taube(n)	pigeon, dove
das Insekt(en)	insect	**der Adler(-)**	eagle
die Spinne(n)	spider		
der Falter(-)	butterfly	**die Biene(n)**	bee
der Schmetterling(e)	butterfly	**die Wespe(n)**	wasp
		die Ameise(n)	ant
das Eichhörnchen(-)	squirrel	**die Schnecke(n)**	snail

Exercises:

Read through the next page before tackling the following exercises:
Talk about your favourite animals and those you don't like. ('Schlangen'? 'Spinnen'?)
Which animal(s) would you most like to have?
Which animals are intelligent and which make a lot of work? ('Arbeit machen')

THE TRANSLATION OF 'TO'

'to' can be **zu**	Wie komme ich **zum Park, zur Kirche zum Hotel?**	
or **nach**	With named geographical locations. Ich fahre **nach** Berlin.	
Two idioms to remember:	Wir gehen **nach Haus(e).**	We are going home.
	Ich bin **zu Haus(e).**	I am at home.

EXPRESSING LIKES, DISLIKES and PREFERENCES

- **Expressing likes or dislikes:**

'gefallen'	conveys visual, aesthetic appreciation or liking Diese Farbe (colour) **gefällt mir (nicht)**. Diese Schuhe **gefallen mir** (nicht). I like/don't like this colour, these shoes.
'schmecken'	denotes liking re. food and drink Sauerkraut **schmeckt mir (nicht).** Muscheln **schmecken mir (nicht).**
Ich hätte gern... **Ich möchte gern...**	I would/should like ... I would/should like (When you are choosing something.) **Ich hätte gern ein Paar Schuhe.** **Ich möchte gern braune Sandalen.**
'mögen' **'gern haben'**	to like, be fond of (in general terms) to like, be fond of (in general terms) **Ich mag Fisch (nicht).** **Mögen Sie Sport?** **Ich habe Sauerkraut gern/nicht gern.**
'gern'	after verbs i.e. to like doing something **Wir schwimmen gern/nicht gern.** **Kochen Sie gern?**

- **Expressing preferences:**

'lieber'	prefer to, would rather Ich koche nicht gern, **ich esse lieber**.
'am liebsten'	best of all **Am liebsten esse ich** Wiener Schnitzel.

- **Expressing an opinion:**

'finden'	**Ich finde** den Bikini **schön/nicht schön.** Finden Sie diesen Film interessant? Wir finden unseren Deutschkurs gut.	
'denken'	**Was denken Sie?**	What do you think?
'glauben'	**Was glauben Sie?**	What do you think (also believe)?

- **DIE FREIZEIT** (Extension to Chapter 12) **LEISURE**

Mein Hobby ist ...
Ich bin sportlich (unsportlich).
Ich bin musikalisch (unmusikalisch).
Ich spiele (play) ein Instrument.

die Geige(n)	violin
das Klavier(e)	piano
die Flöte(n)	flute
das Cello(s)	cello
das Schlagzeug(e)	drums etc.

ich spiele	**Fußball** (football)
ich spiele	**Tennis** (tennis)
ich spiele	**Tischtennis** (tabletennis)
	etc.
ich sammle (collect)	**Marken** (stamps)
ich sammle	**Münzen** (coins)

wir machen	**Gartenarbeit**	we work in the garden
wir machen	**Reisen**	we travel
wir machen	**Ausflüge**	we go on trips
wir machen	**Wanderungen**	we go hiking
wir machen	**Schiffsreisen**	we go on cruises

wir renovieren unser Haus, unsere Wohnung	we renovate, restore ...
wir streichen, tapezieren, lackieren ...	we paint, paper, gloss (varnish) ...
wir machen Holzarbeiten, Handarbeiten	we do woodwork, needlework
wir sehen oft fern	we often watch television
wir lesen Bücher, Zeitungen, Zeitschriften	we read books, newspapers, magazines
wir hören Musik	we listen to music

wir gehen	**spazieren**	we go walking
wir gehen	**wandern**	we go hiking
wir gehen	**schwimmen**	we go swimming
wir gehen	**schifahren**	we go skating
wir gehen	**bergsteigen**	we go climbing
wir gehen	**reiten**	we go riding
wir gehen	**segeln**	we go sailing

wir joggen, laufen (run), **fotografieren, tanzen, kochen** (cook), etc.

Haben Sie ein Hobby?	Do you have a hobby?
Sind Sie sportlich?	Do you like sports?
Sind Sie musikalisch?	Are you musical?
Haben Sie künstlerische Neigungen oder irgendwelche Talente?	Have you artistic inclinations or talents?

• BRIEFE, KARTEN etc. — LETTERS, CARDS, etc.

der Brief(e)	letter
die Karte(n)	card
der Glückwunsch(¨e)	congratulation
die Ansichtskarte(n)	picture postcard
der Gruß(¨e)	greeting
herzlich	sincere
hochachtungsvoll	yours faithfully
geehrt	honoured

- **INFORMAL** when you are on 'Du' terms

- **Dear...**
  Liebe Anna!
  Lieber Paul!
  Liebe Freunde!
  Meine Lieben!

- **Yours sincerely...** — **Yours ...**

Viele Grüße!	Dein John	
Liebe Grüße!	Deine Sabine	
Herzliche Grüße!	Grüße auch an Deine Eltern.	remember me to your parents

- **FORMAL** when you are on 'Sie' terms

- **Dear ...**
  Sehr geehrte Frau Müller!
  Sehr geehrter Herr Müller!
  Sehr geehrtes Fräulein Meier!
  Sehr geehrte Damen und Herrn!

- **Yours sincerely, yours faithfully...** — **Yours**

Mit freundlichen Grüßen!	Ihr/Ihre
Freundliche Grüße!	or
Herzliche Grüße!	name
Hochachtungsvoll!	name only
Empfehlungen auch an Herrn Dr. Ohl	also regards to ...

- **BRIEFE, KARTEN etc.** — **LETTERS, CARDS, etc.**

- **General**

Instead of '!' you can use a ',' but must not start with a capital at the beginning of a letter.

Capitals on 'Du' and 'Sie' and related forms.

Ladies are mentioned first, e.g. 'sehr geehrte **Damen** und Herrn'.

Don't put a capital on 'ich'.

Don't start a sentence with 'ich'.

Always refer to yourself in the second place, e.g. 'Paul und ich ...'

- **Herzlichen Glückwunsch** (congratulations)

zum Geburtstag	birthday
zur Verlobung	engagement
zur Hochzeit	wedding
zum ... Jubiläum	anniversary
zur Promotion	for a doctorate

- **Frohe Weihnachten und viel Glück im neuen Jahr** — Merry Christmas and a Happy New Year
- **Frohe Ostern** — Happy Easter

- **Address** — On the back of the envelope
- **Date** — Personal letters: top right hand corner of letter

  Business letters: variable, depending on printed spaces and preferred format

• AM TELEFON — ON THE PHONE

Hallo!	Hello!
Kann ich Herrn/Frau/Fräulein*..... sprechen?	Can I speak to Mr., Mrs., Miss......?

* 'Fräulein' is only appropriate for fairly young girls up to about late teens. After that the term 'Frau' is used whether the woman is married or not.

am Apparat	speaking
Hier spricht Müller.	(Mr.) Müller speaking.
Müller hier.	ditto
Einen Augenblick (einen Moment)!	One Moment!
Bitte bleiben Sie am Apparat!	Hold on, please!
Bitte warten!	Please wait!
Ich verbinde Sie.	I am putting you through.
falsch verbunden	wrong number
Die Nummer ist besetzt.	The line is engaged.
Herr/Frau/Fräulein .... ist nicht im Büro.	Mr., Mrs., Miss .... is not in the office.
Können Sie später anrufen?	Can you ring later?
Ich rufe um 6 Uhr an.	I shall ring at six o'clock.
Kann ich etwas ausrichten?	Can I pass on a message?
die Vorwählnummer	dialling code
die Vorwahl	ditto
die Direktwahl	direct dialling
die Nebenstelle	extension
die Auskunft	directory enquiries information
die Vermittlung	operator service
das Ortsgespräch	local call
das Inlandgespräch	national call
das Auslandgespräch	international call
das R - Gespräch	reverse-charge call
zum Nulltarif telefonieren	free phone dialling
der Notruf	emergency number

Phone numbers are given as follows:

e.g. 0049 611 52 61 07 — null - null - neunundvierzig - sechshundertelf zweiundfünfzig - einundsechzig - null - sieben

BERUFE und TITEL — JOBS and TITLES

- **General** (see also p.101)

der Chef(s)	boss
der Direktor(en)	head, director
der Leiter(-)	manager
der Arbeitgeber(-)	employer
der Arbeitnehmer(-)	employee
der Beschäftigte(n)	employee
der/dieArbeitslose(n)	unemployed person
der Fachmann(¨er)	expert
der Experte(n)	expert
der Berater(-)	consultant
der Freiberufler(-)	freelance
der Rentner(-)	pensioner
der Pensionist(en)	pensioner

- **Akademische Berufe** graduate professions

der Doktor(en) title after gaining a doctorate in a subject
der Arzt,die Ärztin* doctor (addressed as 'Herr/Frau Doktor')
* '-in' or '-In' ending for the female equivalent in all job titles
der Zahnarzt(¨e) dentist

der Jurist(en) a person qualified at law
der Rechtsanwalt(¨e) lawyer
der Richter(-) judge

der Prokurist(en) accountant
der Steuerberater(-) tax consultant
der Wirtschaftsberater(-) general business/investment/tax consultant
der Finanzberater(-) financial consultant

der Studienrat(¨e) master at a high school
der Lehrer(-) teacher
der Dozent(en) senior/principal lecturer (university)
der Professor(en) professor (university)
(also graduate high school teacher in Austria/Switzerland)
der Architekt(en) architect
der Diplomingenieur(e) highly qualified graduate engineer

- **Das Handwerk** the trades, crafts

der Bäcker(-)	baker
der Fleischer(-)	butcher
der Friseur(e)	airdresser
der Elektriker(-)	electrician
der Mechaniker(-)	mechanic
der Tischler(-)	joiner
der Maschinenschlosser(-)	tool maker
der Zimmermann(¨e)	carpenter
der Maurer(-)	brick layer
der Baumeister(-)	builder
der Klempner(-)	plumber
der Schlosser(-)	locksmith
derMaler(-)/Anstreicher/ Lackierer(-)	painter

BERUFE und TITEL — JOBS and TITLES

- **Das Militär** — the services

das Heer(e)	army	**der Soldat(en)**	soldier
die Armee(n)	army	**der Seemann(¨er)**	sailor
die Marine(n)	navy	**der Matrose (n)**	sailor
die Luftwaffe(n)	airforce	**der Offizier(e)**	officer
die Handelsmarine	merchant navy		

- **Others**

der Handlesvertreter(-)	representative	**die Krankenschwester(n)**	nurse
der Handelsreisende(n)	commercial traveller	**der Krankenpfleger(-)**	male nurse
der Verkäufer(-)	sales assistant	**der Postbote(n)**	postman
		der Briefträger(-)	ditto
der Buchhalter	accountant		
(der Bilanzbuchhalter)		**der Ingenieur(e)**	engineer
der/die Büroangestellte(n)	clerk		
die Sekretärin(nen)	secretary	**der Makler(-)**	broker
		der Immobilienmakler(-)	estate agent
die Röntgenassistentin(nen)	radiographer		
der Polizist(en)	policemen	**der Börsenmakler(-)**	stockbroker
der Fahrer (Führer)	driver	**die Hausfrau(en)**	housewife
der Führer(-)	guide, leader	**das Kindermädchen(-)**	nanny
der Bauer(n)	farmer	**der Koch(¨e)**	cook (m.)
der Landwirt(e)	farmer	**die Köchin(nnen)**	cook (f.)
der Lehrling(e)	apprentice	**der Laborant(en)**	laboratory assistant
der Auszubildende(n) (AZUBI)	trainee		

• WIRTSCHAFT, INDUSTRIE — THE ECONOMY, INDUSTRY

If students come from a business, commercial or industrial background, studying can easily be made more relevant by substituting relevant terminology in a number of chapters for the general core material i.e situations featuring John and friends. 'Introductions' (chapter1) for instance can be adapted to include a business situation with persons listed in the box below.

Instead of talking about houses, where and how people live (chapters 1- 5) one could talk about one's place of employment, what is being produced there, whether one likes the job and colleagues etc. There is a lot of useful information in this section which can be used in a variety of ways.

die Wirtschaft	economy
die Privatwirtschaft	private industry the private sector
die Industrie(n)	industry
der Industriezweig(e)	a branch of industry
die verstaatlichte Industrie	state owned industry
die verarbeitende Industrie	manufacturing industry
der Dienstleistungssektor	service industry
Kommunale Dienste	municipal services

• FIRMEN, ORGANISATIONEN — FIRMS, ORGANISATIONS

der Konzern(e)	large company	**die Abteilung(en)**	department
die Firma(en)	firm, company	**das Büro(s)**	office
das Unternehmen(-)	firm, company	**die Agentur(en)**	agency
der Betrieb(e)	firm, company	**die Vertretung(en)**	agency
das Finanzamt	tax office	**das Amt(¨er)**	government office

das Ministerium(en)	government department, ministry
das Bundesministerium	federal ministry

einen Vertrag abschließen	to conclude a contract
zu Verhandlungen bereit sein	to be ready to negotiate
verhandeln	to negotiate

der Vorstand(¨e)	board of directors	**der Chef(s)**	boss
der Aufsichtsrat(¨e)	supervisory board	**der Direktor(en)**	head, director
der Betriebsrat(¨e)	works committee	**der Leiter(-)**	manager
abstimmen	to vote		

• WIRTSCHAFT, INDUSTRIE — THE ECONOMY, INDUSTRY

der Verkaufsdirektor(en)	sales director
der Geschäftsführer(-)	company secretary
der Personalchef(s)	personel manager
die Chefsekretärin(nen)	p.a. to the director
der Produktionsleiter(-)	production manager
der Marketingleiter(-)	marketing manager
der Prokurist(en)	authorised signatory, accountant
der Sachbearbeiter(-)	person responsible for a specific subject area

der Arbeitgeber(-)	employer	**das Produkt(e)**	product
der Arbeitnehmer(-)	employee	**das Erzeugnis(se)**	product
der Beschäftigte(n)	employee	**der Erzeuger(-)**	producer
		die Erzeugung(en)	production
der Hersteller(-)	producer	**die Herstellung(en)**	production

die Werbung(en)	advertising, marketing
die Arbeit(en)	work
die Verarbeitung(en)	processing
die Fertigung(en)	finishing process
der Arbeitsplatz(¨e)	work place
der Arbeitsmarkt(¨e)	employment situation
die Kurzarbeit(en)	reduced employment
die Krise(n)	crisis
die Einsparung(en)	savings
die Kündigung(en)	redundancy
der Streik(s)	strike
der Wettbewerb(e)	competition
die Konkurrenz	competition
der Konkurrent(en)	competitor
der Absatz(¨e)	sales (of a product)
der Umsatz(¨e)	turnover
die Leistung(en)	performance, output

• WIRTSCHAFT, INDUSTRIE — THE ECONOMY, INDUSTRY

A few useful phrases when introducing your company

Unsere Firma befindet sich in ...	Our company is situated in ...
Wir sind in der Elektronikbranche tätig ...	We deal in electronics...
Wir sind ein gut durchorganisierter und strukturierter Betrieb ...	We are a well organised and structured business ...
Mit hundertzwanzig Mitarbeitern ...	With 120 employees ...
Wir sind aufgeschloßen für ...	We are open to ...
Wir sind jederzeit bereit ...	We are always ready ...
Rufen Sie uns an, unsere Rufnummer ist ...	Call us on ...
Wir beraten Sie jederzeit fachmännisch ...	We offer our expert advice at all times ...
Wir betreuen unsere Kunden ...	We look after our customers ...
Unser Kundendienst ist ausgezeichnet ...	Our service (after sales service) is excellent ...

• GESCHÄFTSKORRESPONDENZ — BUSINESS CORRESPONDENCE

A few key terms (see also LETTERS, CARDS, p.165)

Zu Händen ...	For the attention of ...
Ihr Zeichen ...	Your reference ...
Unser Zeichen ...	Our reference ...
die Anlage(n)	material enclosed
das Datum (Daten)	date
das Schreiben(-)	letter
die Anfrage(n)	enquiry
die Antwort(en)	answer
Bescheid sagen	to inform

- **WIRTSCHAFT, INDUSTRIE** **THE ECONOMY, INDUSTRY**

- **Hoping to set up a deal?** The following list will be useful.

die Ware(n)	product, goods
die Warenpalette(n)	range of goods
die Produktpalette(n)	product range
das Sortiment(s)	choice, range of goods
das Muster(-)	sample
der/das Teil(e)	part, component

das Angebot(e)	offer	**der Handelspartner(-)**	trading partner
anbieten	to offer	**der Außenhandel**	foreign trade
die Anfrage(en)	query	**die Abteilung(en)**	department
anfragen	to ask	**die Entwicklung(en)**	development
bitten	to request	**die Verwaltung(en)**	administration
der Auftrag(¨e)	order	**der Vertrag(¨e)**	contract
die Bestellung(en)	order	**der Entwurf(¨e)**	draft
bestellen	to order	**unterzeichnen**	to sign

der Termin(e)	deadline, also appointment
die Besprechung(en)	small meeting
die Sitzung(en)	meeting

die Tagesordnung(en)	agenda	**der Spediteur(e)**	haulage contractor
die Agenda(s)	agenda	**die Fracht(en)**	freight
das Protokol(le)	minutes	**der Versand**	dispatch

die Messe(n)	fair
die Konferenz(en)	conference
der Treffpunkt(e)	meeting point
treffen (ref.)	to meet
vereinbaren	to arrange

die Zahlungsfrist(en)	the time within which payment has to be made		
Zahlungsbedingungen	conditions of payment		
die Bezahlung(en)	payment		
die Zahlung(en)	payment		
die Lieferung(en)	delivery	**der Kundendienst**	after sales service
der Liefertermin(e)	delivery date	**das Lager(-)**	stock, store
der Lieferant(en)	supplier	**die Lieferfrist(en)**	delivery within a specified time

- **WIRTSCHAFT, INDUSTRIE** — **THE ECONOMY, INDUSTRY**

- **Looking for a job in one of the German speaking countries?**

Stellenanzeigen	job adverts
das Inserat(e)	advertisement
die Anzeige(n)	advertisement
die Stellensuche	situations wanted
die Jobsuche	situations wanted
die Stellenangebote	situations vacant

- **Some job requirements:**

wir suchen	we are looking for
Fachpersonal, Fachkraft(¨e)	personnel with special knowledge in ...
Sachbearbeiter(in)	employee for a particular area of work
Absolvent(in)	a person who has completed his/her training, school, university, etc.
mit Ausbildung in ...	trained for ...
mit Führerschein	able to drive
mit Bereitschaft zu ...	prepared to ...
mit Niveau	high level, of a good standard
mit Interesse an ...	with interest in ...
der Bereich(e)	sector, area
der Dienstleistungsbereich	service sector
der kaufmännische Beruf(e)	job in the commercial sector
der Wirtschaftsberuf(e)	job in the commercial sector
die Verwaltung(en)	administration
die Kostenrechnung(en)	costing
mit Fremdsprachenkenntnissen	with knowledge of foreign languages
mit EDV Kenntnissen	computer literate
Textverarbeitung	word processing
mit Berufserfahrung(en)	professionally experienced
der Verantwortungsbereich(e)	area of responsibility
das Verhandlungsgeschick	negotiating skills
Verträge abschließen	to conclude contracts

• WIRTSCHAFT, INDUSTRIE — THE ECONOMY, INDUSTRY

• Stellenangebote — Job Offers

wir bieten	we are offering
gute Bezahlung	good pay
gute Verdienstmöglichkeiten	good earnings potential
die Dauerstellung	permanent position
die Sozialleistungen	benefits package
vielseitige Tätigkeit	varied work
interessante Tätigkeit	interesting work
gleitende Arbeitszeit	flexi time
die Einschulung	training
die Umschulung	retraining
schriftliche Bewerbung an ...	apply in writing to ...
der Lebenslauf(e)	curriculum vitae
die Terminvereinbarung	arranging an appointment
die Bewerbung(en)	application
das Interview(s)	interview
das Vorstellungsgespräch(e)	interview

- **BANK und FINANZ TERMINOLOGIE** — **BANKING and FINANCE**

die Bank(en)	bank	**der Bürge(n)**	guarantor
das Geldinstitut(e)	ditto	**die Bonität**	creditworthiness
die Bankfiliale(n)	branch	**die Schulden**	debt(s)
die Sparkasse(n)	savings bank	**die Kaution(en)**	down payment (e.g. rent)
die Wechselstube(n)	bureau de change	**die Anzahlung(en)**	down payment (e.g. on property)
der Bankomat(e)	cash point		
		die Rate(n)	instalment
das Geld(er)	money	**der Zins(en)**	interest
der Geldschein(e)	bank note	**der Zinsfuß**	interest rate
die Münze(n)	coin		
das Kleingeld	(small) change	**die Rendite(n)**	return, yield
		der Betrag(¨e)	sum, amount
die Währung(en)	currency	**der Gewinn(e)**	profit
der Devisenkurs(e)	exchange rate		

die deutsche Mark (DM)	German mark
der österreichische Schilling(e) (ö.S.)	Austrian shilling
der schweizer Franken (s.F)	Swiss franc

das Bankkonto(s)	bank account	**(be)zahlen**	to pay
der Kontoauszug(¨e)	bank statement	**einzahlen**	to pay in
		abzahlen	to pay off
ein Konto eröffnen	to open an account	**auszahlen**	to pay out
ein Konto schließen	to close an account		
ein Konto überziehen	to be overdrawn	**sparen**	to save
		schulden	to owe
das Guthaben	balance		
die Buchung	entry	**abheben**	to draw money
der Dauerauftrag(¨e)	standing order	**abbuchen**	to debit
der Bankeinzug(¨e)	direct debit		
die Überweisung(en)	transfer(money)	**begleichen**	to settle (a bill)
der Scheck(s)	cheque	**überweisen**	to transfer (funds)
der Reisescheck(s)	travellers cheque	**bevollmächtigen**	to give authority, power of attorney

kündigen	to cancel, terminate (agreements etc.)
stornieren	to cancel, terminate (payments)

der Scheck ist nicht gedeckt	the cheque has bounced
der Scheck ist geplatzt	ditto
einen Scheck einlösen	to cash a cheque

die Kreditkarte(n)	credit card
der Kredit(e)	credit
die Gebühr(en)	fee
der Vertrag(¨e)	contract, agreement

die Investition(n)	investment
die Geldanlage(n)	ditto
die Aktie(n)	share
der Aktionär(e)	share holder
die Wertpapiere	securities, shares
die Börse(n)	stock exchange
der Makler(-)	broker

• DIE VERSICHERUNG — INSURANCE

die Versicherung(en)	insurance
der Berater(-)	consultant
der Beratungsdienst(e)	advisory service
beraten	to advise
der Schutzbrief(e)	policy
die Police(n)	policy
der Vertrag(¨e)	contract
einen Vertrag abschließen	to conclude (sign) a contract
unterschreiben	to sign
unterzeichnen	ditto
die Bedingung(en)	condition
der Beitrag(¨e)	payment (can also mean'contribution')
die Prämie(n)	payment (can also mean 'bonus')
fällig sein	to be due (payments)
überfällig sein	to be overdue
der Unfall(¨e)	accident
einen Unfall haben	to have an accident
einen Unfall verschulden	to cause an accident
der Notfall(¨e)	emergency
der Schaden(¨en)	damage
der Schadenersatz	compensation, damages
die Reiseversicherung(en)	travel insurance
die Haftpflichtversicherung(en)	indemnity insurance
die Unfallversicherung	accident insurance

- **TECHNISCHE TERMINOLOGIE** (allgemein) — **TECHNICAL TERMS** (general)

- **die Gebrauchsanweisung(en)** instruction manual

• **die Maschine(n)**	**machine**	**die Reparatur(-en)**	**repair**
der Apparat(e)	apparatus	**reparieren**	to repair
das Gerät(e)	appliance	**die Werkstatt(¨en)**	workshop
das Gerät(e)	device	**die Wartung(en)**	maintenance
der Motor(en)	engine	**warten**	to maintain
das Triebwerk(e)	engine (aircraft)	**die Montage(n)**	the fitting of ...
die Ausrüstung(en)	equipment	**montieren**	to fit
die Vorrichtung(en)	device	**die Einstellung(en)**	adjustement
		einstellen	to adjust
• **das Metall(e)**	**metal**	**die Schraube(n)**	**screw**
der Stahl	steel	**der Schraubenschlüssel(-)**	spanner
rostfrei	stainless	**der Schraubenzieher(-)**	screwdriver
das Eisen	iron	**die Mutter(n)**	nut
das Gußeisen	cast iron	**der Bolzen(-)**	bolt
die Gießerei(n)	foundry		
		der Bohrer(-)	**drill**
das Blei	lead	**der Hammer(-)**	hammer
das Kupfer	copper	**die Zange(n)**	pliers
das Messing	brass		
das Blech(e)	sheet metal	**die Schleifmaschine(n)**	sander
der Schrott	scrap metal	**die Säge(n)**	saw
• **der Kraftstoff(e)**	**fuel**	**der Druck(e)**	**pressure**
das Öl(e)	oil	**das Leck(s)**	leak
das Benzin(e)	petrol	**die Dichtung(en)**	seal
		die Pumpe(n)	pump
• **das Wasser(-)**	water	**der Pegel(-)**	level (e.g. water)
die Luft(-)	air		
der Sauerstoff	oxygen	**der Abfall(¨e)**	**waste**
der Wasserstoff	hydrogen	**die Lagerung(en)**	storage
der Stickstoff	nitrogen	**das Lager(-)**	store
• **die Umwelt**	environment	**die Belastung**	affected by pollution
der Müll	rubbish, waste	**das Gift(e)**	poison
die Müllhalde(n)	rubbish tip	**die Wiederverwertung(en)**	recycling
die Müllkippe(n)	ditto	**die Verschmutzung(en)**	pollution
das Kernkraftwerk(e)	atomic power station	**die Kernkraft**	atomic power

- **TECHNISCHE TERMINOLOGIE ctd.** (allgemein) — **TECHNICAL TERMS** (general)

• **der Rohstoff(e)**	**raw materials**		
der Baustoff(e)	building material, constituent		
der Kunststoff(e)	plastic, artificial material		
der Klebstoff(e)	glue		
das Holz(¨er)	wood		
der Stein(e)	stone	**die Platte(n)**	**panel, sheet**
der Schotter(-)	gravel	**das Furnier(e)**	veneer
das Gummi	rubber	**die Paneelplatte(n)**	panelling
die Glasfaser(n)	fibreglass	**das Sperrholz**	plywood
das Harz(e)	resin		
der Teer(e)	tar		
• **die Elektrizität**	**electricity**	**das Rad(¨er)**	**wheel**
der Strom(¨e)	current	**das Zahnrad(¨er)**	cog wheel
der Stromkreis(e)	circuit	**das Schwungrad(¨er)**	fly wheel
die Sicherung(en)	fuse	**das Lenkrad(¨er)**	steering wheel
der Schalter(-)	switch		
die Glühbirne(n)	bulb		
die Spule(n)	coil	**der Schlüssel(-)**	key
der Draht(¨e)	wire	**das Schloß(¨er)**	lock
das Kabel(-)	cable	**schließen**	to shut
die Leitung(en)	duct, mains	**das Scharnier(e)**	hinge
		dieVerriegelung(en)	locking system
• **der Hebel(-)**	**lever**		
der Griff(e)	handle		
		er Schmierstoff(e)	grease
die Kurbel(n)	crank	**schmieren**	to grease
der Knopf(¨e)	button	**das Messer(-)**	**meter, gauge**
die Taste(n)	key	**der Zähler(-)**	counter
die Tastatur(en)	key board	**der Anzeiger(-)**	indicator
• **die Kette(n)**	**chain**	**der Riemen(-)**	**belt**
der Schlauch(¨e)	tube, hose	**der Gurt(e)**	belt
das Rohr(e)	pipe	**der Ventilator(en)**	fan
die Stange(n)	rod		
• **das Gehäuse(-)**	**housing, box**	**der Anstrich(e)**	coat of paint
die Verkleidung(en)	cladding, trim	**der Lack(e)**	varnish
die Beschichtung(en)	coating		

• DER VERKEHRSUNFALL — MOTOR ACCIDENTS

See also: Chapter 16

der Unfall(¨e)	accident	**einen Unfall haben**	to have an accident
der Zusammenstoß(¨sse)	collision	**die Kontrolle über den**	to lose control
die Geschwindigkeit(en)	speed	**Wagen verlieren**	over the car
auf nasser Fahrbahn	on a wet road surface	**(zu) schnell**	(too) fast
		(zu) langsam	(too) slow
der Autofahrer(-)	driver	**kommen** (ist gekommen)	to come
der Beifahrer(-)	passenger	**fahren** (ist gefahren)	to drive
der Fußgänger(-)	pedestrian	**gehen** (ist gegangen)	to go
der Radfahrer(-)	cyclist		
der Motorradf.	motor-cyclist	**überqueren** (hat überquert)	to cross
		halten (hat gehalten)	to stop
die Ampel(n)	traffic lights	**bremsen** (hat gebremst)	to brake
die Ecke(n)	corner		
um die Ecke	round the corner	**parken** (hat geparkt)	to park
		wenden (hat gewendet)	to turn
die Kreuzung(en)	crossroads	**reversieren**	to reverse
das Verkehrszeichen(-)	traffic sign	**nicht mehr halten**	not able to
das Warnschild(er)	warning sign	**(bremsen)können**	stop (brake)
die Autobahn(en)	motorway	**in die Kurve fahren**	to take a bend
das Autobahnkreuz(e)	motorway junction		
die Ausfahrt	exit	**einordnen**	to get in lane
die Einfahrt, Auffahrt	feeder road	(hat sich eingeordnet)	
die Standspur(en)	hard shoulder	**überfahren**	to drive over
der Pannenstreifen	ditto	(hat überfahren)	
die Überholspur(en)	fast lane		
der Notruf	emergency phone nr.	**hineinfahren**	to drive into
		(ist hineingefahren)	
der Kilometerstein(e)	distance marker		
die Straße(n)	road	**anfahren**	to drive into
die Bundesstraße(n)	A - road	(hat angefahren)	
die Einbahnstraße(n)	one way street	**niederfahren**	to mow down
		(hat niedergefahren)	
der Führerschein(e)	driving licence		
die Wagenpapiere	car documents	**schleudern**	to skid
		(hat geschleudert)	
die Versicherung(en)	insurance	**versichert sein**	to be insured
die Gefahr(en)	danger	**gefährlich**	dangerous

DER VERKEHRSUNFALL

MOTOR ACCIDENTS

See also: Chapter 16

die Verletzung(en)	injury	**verletzt sein**	to be injured
der Krankenwagen	ambulance	**ins Krankenhaus bringen** (hat gebracht)	to take to hospital

abbiegen (ist abgebogen von)	to turn off
einbiegen (ist eingebogen in)	to turn into
einsteigen (ist eingestiegen in)	to get into
aussteigen (ist ausgestiegen aus)	to get out of

an	at, on	**bis zu**	up to
auf	on, at	**über**	across, over
bei	near, at	**vor**	in front of
mit	with	**hinten**	at the back of

For additional useful information consult the vocabulary provided with chapter16 and the picture ' EINE DEUTSCHE STADT ' (Chapter 5) .

Body		Karosserie
Bonnet	**1**	Motorhaube
Front wing	**2**	Vorderer Koftflügel
Front valance	**3**	Querfrontblech
Grille	**4**	Kühlergrill
Roof panel	**5**	Dachblech
Windscreen sealing rubber	**6**	Scheibendichtung
Trim moulding	**7**	Zierleiste
Windscreen	**8**	Windschutzscheibe
Tyre	**9**	Reifen
Wheel	**10**	Rad
Hub cap	**11**	Radkappe
Read door	**12**	Hintertür
Front door	**13**	Vordertür
Side sill	**14**	Türschwelle
Door mirror	**15**	Aussenspiegel
Rear window glass	**16**	Heckscheibe
Rubber seal	**17**	Scheibendichtung
Rear wing	**18**	Hinterer Kotflügel
Front bumper	**19**	Vordere Stoβstange
Front overrrider	**20**	Vord. Stoβstangenhorn
Number plate	**21**	Nummernschild
Headlamp rim	**22**	Scheinwerfereinfassung
Headlamp	**23**	Scheinwerfer
Indicator front right/left	**24**	Blinker vorn, rechts/links
Indicator rear right/left	**24A**	Blinker hinten rechts/links
Side light	**25**	Parkleuchte
Stop and tail light	**26**	Brems- und Rüchleuchte
Stop and tail light glass	**27**	Glas, Brems- und Rückleuchte
Reflector	**28**	Reflektor
Rear number plate light	**29**	Nummerschildleuchte
Rear bumper	**30**	Hintere Stoβstange

Plastic//rubber pipe	Kunstoff-/Gummischlauch
Draht	
Nut	Mutter
Bolt	Bolzen
Washer	Unterlagsscheibe
Screw	Schraube
Spanner	Schraubenschlüssel
Screwdriver	Schraubenzieher
Soft wire	Weichdraht
Clip	Schlauchklemme
Fuse	Sicherung
Plier	Zange

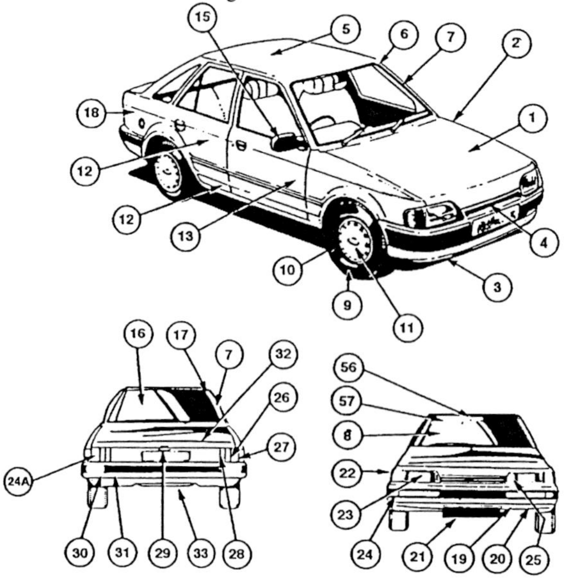

Das Auto

the drive shaft	Antriebswelle
the rear axle	Hinterachse
the fuses have blown	die Sicherungen sind durchgebrannt

- **KRIMINALTERMINOLOGIE** **CRIME and some LEGAL TERMINOLOGY**

Reading is the way to increase fluency in a foreign language once one has learnt the basics. You might get the chance to pick up a German, Austrian or Swiss paper or magazine either in class, at an airport passing the time or perhaps in one of the German speaking countries. Trying to extract information from interesting looking articles, dealing perhaps with crime, would be very frustrating as the relevant terminology is not usually found in German books for beginners. Recourse to the vocabulary below is the answer, yet another reason to keep your German book at hand at all times!
Rôle play is not necessarily suggested here!!

• **das Verbrechen(-)**	crime		
der Verbrecher(-)	criminal		
der Dieb(e)	thief	**stehlen**	to steal
der Diebstahl	theft		
der Mord(e)	murder	**morden**	to murder
der Mörder(-)	murderer	**töten**	to kill
der Einbruch(¨e)	break in, burglary	**einbrechen**	to break in
der Einbrecher(-)	burglar		
der Überfall(¨e)	attack	**überfallen**	to attack
die Gewalt(en)	violence		
die Vergewaltigung(en)	rape	**vergewaltigen**	to rape
• **die Polizei**	police	**festnehmen (s.)**	to apprehend
		überwältigen	to overpower
der Polizist(en)	policeman	**verhören**	to interrogate
die Wachstube(n)	police station	**abführen (s.)**	to lead away
der Polizeiauto	police car		
der Streifenwagen(-)	patrol car		
der Zeuge(n)	witness		
die Aussage(n)	statement		
eine Anzeige machen	to bring a charge against somebody		
• **das Gericht(e)**	court		
der Richter(-)	judge		
der Anwalt(¨e)	advocat	**anklagen**	to indict, charge
die Anklage(n)	indictment, charge		
das Urteil(e)	sentence, judgement	**verurteilen**	to sentence
die Strafe(n)	fine	**strafen**	to fine, punish
das Gefängnis(se)	prison	**einsperren (s.)**	to lock up

GRAMMAR SURVEY

THE ARTICLE

The definite article 'the' and the indefinite article 'a'.

		der (m.)	der Elefant, der Garten, der Mann
the	can be either	**die (f.)**	die Hand, die Rose, die Frau
		das (n.)	das Buch, das Glas, das Kind

'der' is called the 'masculine', 'die' the 'feminine' and 'das' the 'neuter' definite article.
'ein' is called the 'masculine', 'eine' the 'feminine' and 'ein' the 'neuter' indefinite article.

		ein (m.)	ein Elefant, ein Garten, ein Mann
'a'	can be either	**eine (f.)**	eine Hand, eine Rose, eine Frau
		ein (n.)	ein Buch, ein Glas, ein Kind

**'der' is called the 'masculine', 'die' the 'feminine' and 'das' the 'neuter' definite article.
'ein' is called the 'masculine', 'eine' the 'feminine' and 'ein' the 'neuter' indefinite article.**

ein a, one **kein** no (not a.........)

'the' in the plural is fortunately just one word: 'die' as in 'die Gärten', 'die Männer'.

NOUNS

Are always one of three 'genders': masculine (m.), feminine (f.) or 'neuter' (n.).
They always begin with a capital letter in German.

der(ein) Elefant	die(eine) Rose	das(ein)Glas
m.	f.	n.

Noun endings vary in the plural, they can be -e, -en, -n, -er, -er, -s or no ending.

There is often an 'Umlaut' in the plural e.g. 'der Garten', 'die Gärten'.
In the vocabulary this is shown in brackets along with the plural ending.

POSSESSIVE ADJECTIVES

sg.						pl.				
mein	**dein**	**Ihr**	**sein**	**ihr**	**sein**	**unser**	**euer**	**Ihr**	**ihr**	f. familiar
my	your f.	your p.	his	her	its	our	your f.	your p.	their	p. polite

For more advanced students: see also Table of Cases, p.197.

THE NOMINATIVE CASE

Used for the so-called subject of a sentence, i.e the person or thing which with the verb makes up the core meaning of a sentence.

Der junge Mann geht mit seinem Hund in den Park.
subject verb

sg.			pl.
m.	f.	n.	all genders
der groß**e** Garten	die groß**e** Stadt	das groß**e** Haus	die groß**en** Häuser
ein groß**er** Garten	eine groß**e** Stadt	ein groß**es** Haus	keine groß**en** Häuser

The possessive adjectives: 'mein', 'dein' etc. follow the same pattern as 'ein' and 'kein'.
'Mein groß**er** Garten'... etc.

THE ACCUSATIVE CASE

sg.			pl.
m.	f.	n.	all genders
den groß**en** Garten	die groß**e** Stadt	das groß**e** Haus	die groß**en** Häuser
ein**en** groß**en** Garten	eine groß**e** Stadt	ein groß**es** Haus	keine groß**en** Häuser

'der' ⇒ **'den'**
changes to
'ein' ⇒ **'einen'**

For the direct object in a sentence: Der Mann sieht **den** Park (ein**en** Park)
subject verb object

after the following prepositions: **durch** (through) **ohne** (without) **für** (for) **um** (around) **gegen** (against) **entlang** (along)

Der Mann geht **durch den** (ein**en**) Park

and when movement (→) is implied after: **in** (in) **auf** (on) **an** (at) **neben** (next to) **vor** (in front of) **hinter** (at the back of) **unter** (under) **ober** (above) **über** (above) **zwischen** (between)

Der Mann geht **in den** (ein**en**) Garten
(The man goes → into the (a) garden)

The accusative change only affects the masculine article **'der'**and **'ein'.**
(See also Grammar Survey p.197, Table of Cases.)

THE DATIVE CASE

sg. m.	sg. f.	sg. n.	pl. all genders
dem groß**en** Garten	**der** groß**en** Stadt	**dem** groß**en** Haus	**den** groß**en** Häuser**n**
ein**em** groß**en** Garten	ein**er** groß**en** Stadt	ein**em** groß**en** Haus	kein**en** groß**en** Häuser**n**

sg.

m.			f.			n.		
der	⇒	**dem**	die	⇒	**der**	das	⇒	**dem**
ein	⇒	ein**em**	eine	⇒	ein**er**	ein	⇒	ein**em**

pl.

die	⇒	**den**
kein	⇒	kein**en**

For the indirect object after dative verbs:

Der Vater	gibt	**dem** Kind	einen Ball.
Nominative	verb	Dative	Accusative
subject		indirect object	direct object

Note the word order in the example above, in English the accusative would come before the dative: The father gives the ball to the child. In German it is the other way round.

Dative verbs

No 'zu' is required (see example above), **just the dative form of the following noun or pronoun.**

sagen	to say	**danken**	to thank
erzählen	to tell	**geben**	to give
berichten	to report	**helfen**	to help
antworten	to answer	**folgen**	to follow
schreiben	to write	**erlauben**	to allow
senden	to send	**gestatten**	to permit
schicken	to send	**dienen**	to serve
zeigen	to show	**raten**	to advise

After dative prepositions:

mit (with) **zu** (to) **aus** (out of, from) **bei** (nearby, at) **nach** (after, past) **von** (from) **seit** (since) **gegenüber** (opposite).

When no movement is implied after: **in** (in) **auf** (on) **an** (at) **neben** (next to) **vor** (in front of) **hinter** (at the back of) **unter** (under) **ober** (above) **über** (above) and **zwischen** (between)

All endings on adjectives are **'-en'** mit **dem** rot**en** Bus in **der** lang**en** Straße

GENITIVE or POSSESSIVE CASE: Translated by 'of the', 'of a'.

das Buch

sg.			pl.
m.	f.	n.	
des jungen Mannes	**der** deutschen Frau	**des** kleinen Kindes	**der** kleinen Kinder
eines jungen Mannes	**einer** deutschen Frau	**eines** kleinen Kindes	**meiner** kleinen Kinder

the book

of the(a) young man	of the(a) German woman	of the(a) small child	of the small children
the(a) young man's book	the(a) German woman's b.	the small child's book	of my small children

sg.

m.			f.			n.		
der	⇒	**des**	die	⇒	**der**	das	⇒	**des**
ein	⇒	eines	eine	⇒	einer	ein	⇒	eines

pl.

die	⇒	**der**
kein	⇒	keiner

The Genitive is also always used after:

(an)statt instead of **trotz** inspite of **wegen** because of **während** during **hinsichtlich** in view of **bezüglich** referring to

PRONOUNS and their CASES

	sg.						pl.			
	I	you*	you+	he	she	it	we	you*	you+	they
Nom.	**ich**	**du**	**Sie**	**er**	**sie**	**es**	**wir**	**ihr**	**Sie**	**sie**
Acc.	**mich**	**dich**	**Sie**	**ihn**	**sie**	**es**	**uns**	**euch**	**Sie**	**sie**
Dat.	**mir**	**dir**	**Ihnen**	**ihm**	**ihr**	**ihm**	**uns**	**euch**	**Ihnen**	**Ihnen**

* familiar + polite

Word order:

Er zeigt **ihm** den Park, die Stadt, das Haus. He shows him the park, the town, the house.
D. A. Position of accusative and dative in a pronoun/noun situation.

Er zeigt **es ihm.** He shows it to him. .
A. D. Position of accusative and dative in a pronoun/ pronoun situation.

It is in fact the same in English, 'him', 'me' etc.being the remnants of the old case structure rooted in the original language from which German and English developed.

THE VERB

e.g. kommen to come

This, the basic form of the verb, is called **the Infinitive**.

The Present Tense (see also TENSES)

Take away the infinitive ending -en and add whichever ending you need (see below).

singular (re.one person or thing)		**plural** (re. several persons or things)	
ich komm**e**	I come (am coming)	wir komm**en**	we come (are coming)
du komm**st**	you come (are coming)	ihr komm**t**	you come (are coming)
Sie komm**en**	you come (polite form)	Sie komm**en**	you come (polite form)
er	he		
sie komm**t**	she comes (is coming)	sie komm**en**	they come (are coming)
es	it		

Verbs with stems ending in 't' or 'd' like warten (to wait), arbeiten (to work), finden (to find) or senden (to send) **need an -et ending instead of just a -t** in the 'er', 'sie', 'es' form e.g. er wartet, er findet. This helps to make pronunciation easier.

There are no -ing forms in German, the continuity of an action is expressed by the simple verb form only e.g. 'Ich komme jetzt' means 'I am coming now' or 'I come now'.

THE AUXILIARIES so-called because they help to form tenses with other verb forms

In English you would use e.g 'to have' not just to denote possession but with the past participle of another verb to form a tense: We have forgotten ....
(aux.) (past participle)

sein to be

ich bin	I am	**wir sind**	we are	Sie sind....	You are....
du bist	you are (f.)	**ihr seid**	you are	Sind Sie...?	Are you...?
Sie sind	you are (p.)	**Sie sind**	you are		
er	he				
sie ist	she is	**sie sind**	they are		
es	it				

(f.) - familiar form
(p.) - polite form

These will not be marked separately from now on. See Grammar, chapter 1, 'Du', 'Sie'.

We will be using the 'Sie' form mainly, as the conversations are between adults.

haben	to have		
ich habe	I have	**wir haben**	we have
du hast	you have	**ihr habt**	you have
Sie haben	you have	**Sie haben**	you have
er	he		
sie hat	she has	**sie haben**	they have
es	it		

Irregular verbs:

Vowel changes in the 'du' and 'er', 'sie', 'es' forms of some verbs in the present tense are quite common, this is one of the reasons why they are called irregular verbs. See also: List of irregular verbs p.200, second column.

sprechen	ich spreche du sprichst Sie sprechen er sie spricht es	There is no change in the plural present tense forms of irregular verbs.

SEPARABLE VERBS marked (s.)

Many German verbs have separable prefixes i.e. **'weg'**- on **'wegfahren'** (to go away). In the infinitive prefix and verb are one word but in a statement or question the prefix goes to the end of the sentence (see below).

Infinitive		statement	question
wegfahren	(to go away)	Wir **fahren** morgen abend **weg**.	Wann **fahren** wir **weg?**
anrufen	(to phone)	Ich **rufe** in zehn Minuten **an**.	**Rufen** Sie mich **an**?

When separable verbs are used in combination with modal verbs (können, möchten, müssen, sollen, wollen, dürfen and mögen) **prefix and verb stay together**:

Wir **können** am Freitag **wegfahren**. Ich **muß** morgen **anrufen**.

MODAL VERBS

These usually combine with other verbs thus imparting a different slant (mood) to their meaning:
Compare 'we come' (no modal verb present) to 'we can come' (modal verb 'can' present) and you will understand their function.

können to be able, can

ich kann (I can)	**wir können**
du kannst	**ihr könnt**
Sie können	**Sie können**
er	
sie kann	**sie können**
es	

müssen to have to, must

ich muß (I must)	**wir müssen**
du mußt	**ihr müsst**
Sie müssen	**Sie müssen**
er	
sie muß	**sie müssen**
es	

Ich kann morgen nicht **kommen.**
Können Sie den Zug **sehen?**

Ich muß jetzt **telefonieren.**
Wir müssen nach Bonn **fahren.**

Note the position of the second verb at the end of the sentence.

sollen should, ought to

ich soll (I should)	**wir sollen**
du sollst	**ihr sollt**
Sie sollen	**Sie sollen**
er	
sie soll	**sie sollen**
es	

wollen to want (to)

ich will (I want)	**wir wollen**
du willst	**ihr wollt**
Sie wollen	**Sie wollen**
er	
sie will	**sie wollen**
es	

Was soll ich trinken?
Das kannst Du trinken.

Du willst vielleicht Milch.
Ich will lieber Schnaps.

möchten (should) would like

ich möchte	**wir möchten**
du möchtest	**ihr möchtet**
Sie möchten	**Sie möchten**
er	
sie möchte	**sie möchten**
es	

mögen to like, be fond of (also 'may')

ich mag	**wir mögen**
du magst	**ihr mögt**
Sie mögen	**sie mögen**
er	
sie mag	**sie mögen**
es	

'möchten' and **'mögen'** and all other modal verbs **are not followed by 'zu'**

In English one would say: 'I would (should) like **to** go'.
In German you would say: **'Ich möchte gehen'.**

'möchten'	**is used a lot to indicate what you would or would not like (to)..., expressing a desire when making a choice**
'mögen'	**expresses a general liking or fondness** occasionally used in the sense of **'may' or 'might'** das mag sein that may be

In a restaurant:	'ich möchte Fisch'	I would like fish (rather than something else)
whereas:	'ich mag Fisch'	I like fish, I am fond of it

MODAL VERBS (ctd.)

'dürfen' to be allowed to', 'may' (modal verb)

ich darf (I am allowed, I may)	**wir dürfen**	Darf ich hier parken?
du darfst	**ihr dürft**	May I park here?
Sie dürfen	**Sie dürfen**	
er		No, you **must not** park here.*
sie darf	**sie dürfen**	**Nein, Sie dürfen hier nicht parken.**
es		

* **'must not'** is expressed by forms of **'dürfen' + nicht'**

REFLEXIVE VERBS

sich interessieren (für) to be interested (in)

ich interessier	**e**	**mich**	**wir interessier**	**en**	**uns**
du	**st**	**dich**	**ihr "**	**t**	**euch**
Sie "	**en**	**sich**	**Sie "**	**en**	**sich**
er					
sie "	**t**	**sich**	**sie "**	**en**	**sich**
es					

sich waschen	to wash	**sich rasieren**	to shave
sich anziehen(s.)	to dress	**sich ausziehen(s.)**	to undress
sich freuen auf...	to look forward to...	**sich freuen über...**	to be pleased about...
sich erinnern an...	to remember	**sich ärgern über...**	to be annoyed about...

THE IMPERATIVE

If you wanted to tell someone to do something e.g. to go or to drive you would use the so-called 'command form' i.e. the imperative.
You would say e.g.: **Go** straight on! **Drive** round the corner!

In German you add a 'Sie' for the polite form:
Gehen Sie links! **Fahren Sie** um die Ecke! 'Sie' form (sg. and pl.)

Geh geradeaus! **Fahr** um die Ecke! 'Du' form, no ending (sg.)
Geht geradeaus! **Fahrt** um die Ecke! 't' ending (pl.)

TENSES

THE PRESENT TENSE

Take away the infinitive ending -en and add whichever ending you need (see below).

singular (re. one person or thing)		**plural** (re. several persons or things)	
ich komme	I come (am coming)	wir komm**en**	we come (are coming)
du komm**st**	you come (are coming)	ihr komm**t**	you come (are coming)
Sie komm**en**	you come (polite form)	Sie komm**en**	you come (polite form)
er	he		
sie komm**t**	she comes (is coming)	sie komm**en**	they come (are coming)
es	it		

Verbs with stems ending in 't' or 'd' like warten (to wait), arbeiten (to work), finden (to find) or senden (to send) **need an -et ending instead of just a -t** in the 'er', 'sie', 'es' form e.g. er wartet, er findet. This helps to make pronunciation easier.
There are no -ing forms in German, the continuity of an action is expressed by the simple verb form only e.g. 'Ich komme jetzt' means 'I am coming now' or 'I come now'.

THE IMPERFECT TENSE

The imperfect or simple past tense ('simple' because there is no auxiliary verb like e.g. 'haben' present, see Perfect tense below) is used in the narrative sense to talk about past events, just like the Perfect. It is used in a slightly more formal context i.e. in the written language whereas the Perfect tends to be used more in the spoken language, particularly in the South of Germany and Austria.

The name 'imperfect' does not imply an incomplete action as is the case in other languages.

How to form the Imperfect Tense:

regular verbs*		**irregular verbs****	
lachen - to laugh		**kommen** - to come	
ich lach**te**	(I laughed)	ich kam	(I came)
du lach**test**	etc.	du kam**st**	etc.
Sie lach**ten**		Sie kam**en**	
er		er	
sie lach**te**		sie kam	
es		es	
wir lach**ten**		wir kam**en**	
ihr lach**tet**		ihr kam**t**	
Sie lach**ten**		Sie kam**en**	
sie lach**ten**		sie kam**en**	

* An 'e' is inserted if the stem ends in 'd' or 't': warten - wart**ete**
** For the imperfect forms of other irregular verbs see p.200, third column.

Most verbs are regular (sometimes called 'weak') and take the '-te' endings as shown below. If you are unsure whether a verb is regular or not check in the list of irregular verbs.

regular verbs

Imperfect		Infinitive	
sagte	said	sagen	to say
wartete	waited	warten	to wait
kaufte	bought	kaufen	to buy
brauchte	needed	brauchen	to need
fragte	asked	fragen	to ask
machte	made	machen	to make, do
rasierte	shaved	rasieren (r.)	to shave
merkte	noticed	merken	to notice
neckten	teased	necken	to tease
lachten	laughed	lachen	to laugh
freuten	looked forward	freuen (r.)	to look forward

Irregular verbs (sometimes called 'strong') are listed separately further on. It is a good idea to try to remember the forms of the more commonly used ones (see below).

These verbs very often show a **stem vowel change** as is also the case in English, e.g. to 'find' but the imperfect or past tense form is 'found'.

irregular verbs

Imperfect		Infinitive	
hatte	had	haben	to have
war	was	sein	to be
begann	began	beginnen	to start, begin
ging	went	gehen	to go
fuhr	travelled	fahren	to travel
stand	stood	stehen	to stand
saß	sat	sitzen	to sit
kam	came	kommen	to come
wußte	knew	wissen	to know
traf	met	treffen	to meet
zog sich um	changed	umziehen	to change
fand	found	finden	to find
wusch	washed	waschen	to wash
trank	drank	trinken	to drink
sprach	spoke, talked	sprechen	to speak, talk

Modal verbs: Their endings follow the regular pattern, some do, however, change their stem vowels.

dürfen	**durfte**	was allowed to
können	**konnte**	could
müssen	**mußte**	had to
sollen	**sollte**	should (have)
mögen	**mochte**	liked
wollte	**wollte**	wanted

THE FUTURE TENSE

The first of the composite tenses i.e. made up of two parts.

forms of werden + infinitive (see below)	**ich werde kommen**	I shall/will come I shall be/will be coming
	ich werde am Montag kommen	note the position of the infinitive 'kommen'.

More about verb combinations: WORD ORDER

'werden' (shall, will)	not to be confused with	**'würden'** (would)	
ich werde	**wir werden**	**ich würde**	**wir würden**
du wirst	**ihr werdet**	**du würdest**	**ihr würdet**
Sie werden	**Sie werden**	**Sie würden**	**Sie würden**
er		**er**	
sie wird	**sie werden**	**sie würde**	**sie würden**
es		**es**	

THE PERFECT TENSE (I)

The perfect tense is formed by the forms of the auxiliary verb 'haben' and the past participle of a verb.

regular verbs
e.g.lachen (to laugh)

	auxilliary	past participle
ich	**habe**	**gelacht**
du	**hast**	**gelacht**
Sie	**haben**	**gelacht**
er		
sie	**hat**	**gelacht**
es		

etc.

I have laughed, I laughed

irregular verbs
e.g.finden

	auxilliary	past participle
ich	**habe**	**gefunden**
du	**hast**	**gefunden**
		etc.

Stem vowels often change in this group, one of the reasons why they are called 'irregular' ('strong') verbs.

More information about this group of verbs in Chapter 15.

I have found, I found

When talking about the past, the perfect tense is often used not just for talking about events that have just happened (as is the case in English) but also about what happened a long time ago.

A German speaker would quite happily say: "Ich habe vor 30 Jahren in Berlin gelebt und habe dort mein Deutsch gelernt." This tense can therefore be used in the narrative sense whenever you want to talk about the past. It adds a note of liveliness to your account.

Some regular past participles:		Some irregular past participles:	
telefoniert*	telefonieren	**begonnen**	beginnen
studiert	studieren	**gesehen**	sehen
gefragt	fragen	**gekommen**	kommen
gesagt	sagen	**gefunden**	finden
gelacht	lachen	**getrunken**	trinken
geantwortet**	antworten	**gegessen**	essen
gewartet**	warten		
gemacht	machen		
verabredet***	verabreden		
verneint***	verneinen	(See: List of Irregular Verbs)	

* verbs ending in -'ieren' do not have a 'ge'- prefix.

** when the verb stem ends in 't' an 'e' is inserted before the ending 't'.

*** verbs starting with unstressed syllables like 'ver'-, 'ent'-, 'be'-, 'emp'-, 'zer'-, 'er'-, 'ge'-, do not prefix with 'ge'- on the past participle.

THE PERFECT TENSE (II)

Verbs of movement and a few others * form the perfect tense with 'sein' instead of 'haben'.

Below is a list of verbs frequently used.

		sg.	
gehen	go	**ich bin gegangen**	**I have gone** or I went
laufen	run, walk	**du bist gelaufen**	**you have run** or you ran
fahren	drive, travel	**Sie sind gefahren**	**you have driven** or drove
kommen	come	**er ist gekommen**	**he has come** or came
fallen	fall	**sie ist gefallen**	**she has fallen** or fell
springen	jump	**es ist gesprungen**	**it has jumped** or jumped
		pl.	
fliegen	to fly	**wir sind geflogen**	**we have flown** or flew
bleiben*	to stay	**ihr seid geblieben**	**you have stayed** or stayed
werden*	to become	**sie sind geworden**	**you have become** or became
sein*	to be	**sie sind gewesen**	**they have been** or were
rennen	to run, race	**ist gerannt**	**has run,** ran
schwimmen	to swim	**ist geschwommen**	**has swum,** swam
wachsen	to grow	**ist gewachsen**	**has grown,** grew
sterben*	to die	**ist gestorben**	**has died,** died
passieren*	to happen	**ist passiert**	**Wann ist das passiert?**
geschehen*	to happen	**ist geschehen**	**Wie ist das geschehen?**
aufstehen (s.)	to get up	**ist aufgestanden**	**has got up,** got up
einsteigen (s.)	to get into	**ist eingestiegen**	**has got into** e.g. a car
aussteigen (s.)	to get out	**ist ausgestiegen**	**has got out** of ditto

WORD ORDER

main clause

Ich **habe** ein gutes Hotel **gefunden**. Wir **sind** in ein Konzert **gegangen.**	Past participle at the end.

subordinate clause

.........., **weil** ich ein gutes Hotel **gefunden habe**.	Auxiliary at the end.
.........., **da** wir mit dem Bus **gefahren sind.**	Auxiliary at the end.
.........., **daß** er das Buch **mitgebracht hat**.	In separable verbs the 'ge-' goes between prefix and verb.

(See also the complete section on **WORD ORDER** at the end of the Grammar Survey)

THE PLUPERFECT TENSE (I)

This tense is formed by combining the forms of 'hatten' with a past participle.

ich	**hatte**	gekauft (I had bought)	wir	**hatten**	gefunden
du	**hattest**	gesagt	ihr	**hattet**	gemacht
Sie	**hatten**	gefragt	Sie	**hatten**	telefoniert
er sie es	**hatte**	begonnen	sie	**hatten**	getrunken

John hatte eine englische Zeitung **gekauft**. (statement)
Er hatte ein ideales Mädchen **gefunden**. (statement)
Er hatte sich auf eine Bank **gesetzt**. (reflexive)

Hatte er sie vielleicht **verloren**? (question)
Ich hatte mich mit .... **verabredet**. (reflexive)
Weil er sich auf eine Bank **gesetzt hatte.** (sub.clause)

(The same principles apply to Pluperfect II. See also WORD ORDER)

THE PLUPERFECT (II)

The verbs listed on p.194 (PERFECT TENSE II) as well as all other verbs of movement and a few others combine with **'war'** instead of 'hatte' to form the pluperfect.

sg.

e.g. kommen	ich	**war**	gekommen	I	**had**	come
	du	**warst**	gekommen	you	**had**	come
	Sie	**waren**	gekommen	you	**had**	come
	er sie es	**war**	gekommen	he she it	**had**	come

pl.

wir	**waren**	gekommen	we	**had**	come
ihr	**wart**	gekommen	you	**had**	come
Sie	**waren**	gekommen	you	**had**	come
sie	**waren**	gekommen	they	**had**	come

The following separable prefixes are often added to verbs of movement to give directional emphasis:

hin-	away from the speaker	**hinein-, herein-**	into
her-	towards the speaker	**hinaus-, heraus-**	out of, from
weg-	away	**ab-**	off, away
vorbei-	past		

e.g. **hinfahren, herkommen, weggehen, vorbeifahren, abfliegen, abfahren**

Mein Bruder studiert in Berlin, ich bin **hingefahren**.
Dein Chef ist hier, du bist **hergekommen**.

Der Park war nicht offen, sie ist **weggegangen**.
Ein super Auto ist **vorbeigefahren**.

Concorde ist vor zwei Stunden **abgeflogen**.
Der Intercity ist gerade **abgefahren**.

COMPARATIVE and SUPERLATIVE

		Comparative		**Superlative**	
schön	beautiful	schön**er**	more beautiful	**am** schön**sten**	most beautiful
klein	small	klein**er**	smaller	**am** klein**sten**	smallest
gut	good	bess**er**	better	**am** best**en**	best of all
hoch	high	höh**er**	higher	**am** höch**sten**	highest

There is no 'more' and 'most' in German comparisons, as in 'more' and 'most beautiful' just 'schöner' and am 'schönsten'.

Comparatives and Superlatives can be used as adjectives: 'der kleinere Apfel', 'der kleinste Apfel' but 'der Apfel ist am kleinsten'.

CASES

ARTICLES ('der' and 'ein' pattern) - NOUNS - ADJECTIVES and their endings

	sg. m.	sg. f.	sg. n.		pl. all genders
NOM	**der** große Park	**die** alte Stadt	**das** kleine Haus	(Nominative)	**die** kleinen Häuser
	ein groß**er Park**	**eine** alte Stadt	**ein** klein**es** Haus		**keine** alten Häuser
ACC	**den** groß**en Park**	**die** alte Stadt	**das** kleine Haus	(Accusative)	**die** kleinen Häuser
	einen groß**en** Park	**eine** alte Stadt	**ein** kleines Haus		**keine** alten Häuser
DAT	**dem** groß**en Park**	**der** alten Stadt	**dem** kleinen Haus	(Dative)	**den** kleinen Häusern+
	einem groß**en Park**	**einer** alten Stadt	**einem** kleinen Haus		**keinen** alten Häusern+
GEN	**des** groß**en** Park(e)s*	**der** alten **Stadt**	**des** kleinen Hauses*	(Genitive)	**der** kleinen Häuser
	eines groß**en** Park(e)s*	**einer** alten Stadt	**eines** kleinen Hauses*		**keiner** alten Häuser

* - (e)s ending on masculine and neuter nouns   + - (e)n noun endings in the dative plural

The same pattern of endings as with 'ein' and 'kein': **'mein', 'dein' etc.**
e.g. 'Mein groß**er** Garten'... etc

The same pattern of endings as with 'der', 'die', 'das' (see table)

dieser, diese, dieses this, this one
jeder, jene, jenes that, that one
jeder, jede, jedes each, every one
welcher, welche, welches which, which one
e.g. Dieser groß**e** Garten ....

Prepositions followed by D Dative, A Accusative, G Genitive, D/A Dative: without movement, Accusative: with movement

an	D/A	at	**gegenüber**	A	opposite	**über**	D	over, across, about
auf	D/A	on, onto	**hinter**	D/A	behind	**um**	A	around
(an)statt	G	instead (of)	**in**	D/A	in	**unter**	D/A	under
aus	D	out of, from	**mit**	D	with	**von**	D	of, from
bei	D	nearby, at	**nach**	D	after, past	**vor**	D/A	in front of
bezüglich	G	refering to	**neben**	D/A	next to	**während**	G	during
durch	A	through	**ober**	D/A	above	**wegen**	G	because
entlang	A	along	**ohne**	A	without	**zwischen**	D/A	between
für	A	for	**seit**	D	since	**zu**	D	to
gegen	A	against	**trotz**	G	in spite of			

WORD ORDER

Main Clause Word Order in Statements

1. **Verb - always the second element**

1	2		
Mein Vater	**kommt** (verb)	morgen.	My father comes tomorrow.
Morgen	**kommt** (verb)	mein Vater.	Tomorrow comes my father - this is where it differs from English (see also next example).

Morgen nach dem Fußballmatch (1) **kommt** (2) mein Vater.

(Even if the first element is quite long, the verb still has to follow as the second element.)

2. **Verb Combinations -** **the auxiliary or modal verb is the second element, the infinitive or pastparticiple goes to the end.**

Ich **werde** (2, aux.) in Deutschland gutes Bier **trinken.** (inf.)

Morgen **werde** (2, aux.) ich in Deutschland gutes Bier **trinken.** (inf.)

Gestern **habe** (2, aux.) ich Mineralwasser **getrunken.** (past part.)

Am Montag **bin** (2, aux.) ich nach Frankfurt **gekommen.** (past part.)

Im Sommer **kann** (2, modal) ich für zwei Wochen in die Alpen **kommen.** (inf.)

3. After **'und'** and, **'aber'** but, **'oder'** or, **'denn'** because, **'sondern'** but (on the contrary), no change to word order, i.e. everything is as in main clauses above.

4. **Separable verbs** - the prefix goes to the end of the clause.

Der Zug **kommt** in fünf Minuten **an.** (prefix)

WORD ORDER

Subordinate Word Order

1. **Verb at the end of sentence if introduced by one of the following words:**

damit	so that	**wo**	where
daß	that	**weil**	because
da	as, because	**ob**	whether, if
deshalb	therefore	**obwohl**	although
weshalb	for that reason	**obgleich**	although
als	when (in the past)	**bevor**	before
wenn	when (whenever)	**seit(dem)**	since
wann	when (question)	**nachdem**	after
während while			

Ich hoffe, **daß** mein Freund **kommt**.
Ich weiß, **wann** Du morgen nachmittag **kommst**.

Relative clauses introduced by 'der', 'die', 'das' or **'welcher', 'welche', 'welches'** or any of their case forms, also follow this pattern.

2. **Separable verbs don't separate:**

Es is gut, **wenn** er nicht **mitkommt**.
(sep.verb)

3. **Verb Combinations:**

The auxiliary or modal verb, i.e. the part which takes the endings, **goes to the very end of a subordinate clause. Past participles and infinitives precede them.**

Ich weiß es nicht, **weil** sie nichts **gesagt** **hat**.
(past part.) (aux.)

Ich sehe, **daß** er das Buch **mitgebracht** **hat**.
(past part.) (aux.)

Es ist gut, **wenn** sie uns **helfen** **kann**.
(inf.) (modal)

Weißt du, **daß** du **anrufen** **mußt**?
(inf./sep.verb)(modal)

	GERMAN	VOWEL CHANGE ? 3rd. person sg, present tense	IMPERFECT	PERFECT	ENGLISH
A	**(ab)fahren**	fährt ab	fuhr ab	**ist** abgefahren	depart,leave
	(ab)geben	gibt ab	gab ab	hat abgegeben	give, hand in
	(ab)laden	lädt ab	lud ab	hat abgeladen	unload
	(an)bieten	bietet an	bot an	hat angeboten	offer
	(an)fangen	fängt an	fing an	hat angefangen	begin, start
	(an)greifen	greift an	griff an	hat angegegriffen	touch
	(an)kommen	kommt an	kam an	**ist** angekommen	arrive
	(an)rufen	ruft an	rief an	hat angerufen	phone
	(an)sehen	sieht an	sah an	hat angesehen	look at
	(an)ziehen	zieht (sich) an	zog (sich) an	hat (sich) angezogen	get dressed
	(auf)bleiben	bleibt auf	blieb auf	**ist** augeblieben	stay up late
	(auf)gehen	geht auf	ging auf	**ist** aufgegangen	rise (sun)
	(auf)schreiben	schreibt auf	schrieb auf	hat aufgeschrieben	write down
	(auf)stehen	steht auf	stand auf	**ist** aufgestanden	get up
	(aus)geben	gibt aus	gab aus	hat ausgegeben	spend money
	(aus)gehen	geht aus	ging aus	**ist** ausgegangen	go out
	(aus)sehen	sieht aus	sah aus	hat ausgesehen	look like
	(aus)steigen	steigt aus	stieg aus	**ist** ausgestiegen	get off/out
B	**backen**	bäckt	buk (backte)	hat gebacken	bake
	befinden	befindet sich	befand sich	hat sich befunden	be (situated)
	beginnen	beginnt	begann	hat begonnen	begin
	behalten	behält	behielt	hat behalten	keep
	beissen	beißt	biss	hat gebissen	bite
	bekommen	bekommt	bekam	hat bekommen	get, receive
	besprechen	bespricht	besprach	hat besprochen	discuss
	betreten	betritt	betrat	hat betreten	enter, step in
	bitten	bittet	bat	hat gebeten	ask for
	bleiben	bleibt	blieb	**ist** geblieben	remain, stay
	brechen	bricht	brach	hat gebrochen	break
	brennen	brennt	brannte	hat gebrannt	burn
	bringen	bringt	brachte	hat gebracht	bring
D	**denken**	denkt	dachte	hat gedacht	think
	dürfen	**darf**	durfte	hat gedurft (hat dürfen)	be allowed, may
E	**(ein)laden**	lädt ein	lud ein	hat eingeladen	invite
	(ein)lassen	läßt ein	ließ ein	hat eingelassen	let in
	(ein)schlafen	schläft ein	schlief ein	**ist** eingeschlafen	fall asleep
	(ein)steigen	steigt ein	stieg ein	**ist** eingestiegen	get in/board
	(ein)treffen	trifft ein	traf ein	**ist** eingetroffen	arrive
	(ein)treten	tritt ein	trat ein	**ist** eingetreten	enter
	empfehlen	empfiehlt	empfahl	hat empfohlen	recommend
	erfahren	erfährt	erfuhr	hat erfahren	get to know
	erhalten	erhält	erhielt	hat erhalten	receive
	erkennen	erkennt	erkannte	hat erkannt	recognise
	erschrecken	erschrickt	erschrak	**ist** erschrocken	be frightened
	ertrinken	ertrinkt	ertrank	**ist** ertrunken	drown
	essen	ißt	aß	hat gegessen	eat

	GERMAN	VOWEL CHANGE ? 3rd. person sg, present tense	IMPERFECT	PERFECT	ENGLISH
F	**fahren**	fährt	fuhr	**ist** gefahren	drive, travel
	fallen	fällt	fiel	**ist** gefallen	fall
	fangen	fängt	fing	hat gefangen	catch
	finden	findet	fand	hat gefunden	find
	fliegen	fliegt	flog	**ist** geflogen	fly
	fressen	frißt	frass	hat gefressen	eat (animals)
	frieren	friert	fror	hat gefroren	freeze
G	**geben**	gibt	gab	hat gegeben	give
	gefallen	gefällt	gefiel	hat gefallen	like, please
	gehen	geht	ging	**ist** gegangen	go, walk
	gelingen	gelingt	gelang	**ist** gelungen	succeed
	genießen	genießt	genoß	hat genossen	enjoy
	geschehen	geschieht	geschah	**ist** geschehen	happen
	greifen	greift	griff	hat gegriffen	seize, grip
H	**haben**	hat	hatte	hat gehabt	have
	halten	hält	hielt	hat gehalten	hold
	hängen	hängt	hing	**ist** gehangen	hang
	heben	hebt	hob	hat gehoben	lift
	heißen	heißt	hieß	hat geheißen	be called
	helfen	hilft	half	hat geholfen	help
K	**kennen**	kennt	kannte	hat gekannt	know
	kommen	kommt	kam	**ist** gekommen	come
	können	**kann**	konnte	hat gekonnt (hat können)	can, be able
L	**lassen**	läßt	ließ	hat gelassen	let, leave (something)
	laufen	läuft	lief	**ist** gelaufen	run
	lesen	liest	las	hat gelesen	read
	liegen	liegt	lag	(hat) ist gelegen	lie
M	**messen**	mißt	maß	hat gemessen	measure
	(mit)bringen	bringt mit	brachte mit	hat mitgebracht	bring along
	(mit)nehmen	nimmt mit	nahm mit	hat mitgenommen	take with you
	(mit)kommen	kommt mit	kam mit	**ist** mitgekommen	go with some-one
	mögen	**mag**	mochte	hat gemocht	like
	müssen	**muß**	mußte	hat gemußt (hat müssen)	must, have to
N	**(nach)denken**	denkt nach	dachte nach	hat nachgedacht	ponder
	(nach)sehen	sieht nach	sah nach	hat nachgesehen	check, look up
	nehmen	nimmt	nahm	hat genommen	take
R	**reiten**	reitet	ritt	**ist** geritten	ride
	rennen	rennt	rannte	**ist** gerannt	run
	riechen	riecht	roch	hat gerochen	smell
	rufen	ruft	rief	hat gerufen	call

	GERMAN	VOWEL CHANGE ? 3rd. person sg, present tense	IMPERFECT	PERFECT	ENGLISH
S	**scheinen**	scheint	schien	hat geschienen	seem, shine
	schlafen	schläft	schlief	hat geschlafen	sleep
	schlagen	schlägt	schlug	hat geschlagen	hit
	schließen	schließt	schloß	hat geschloßen	close
	schneiden	schneidet	schnitt	hat geschnitten	cut
	schreiben	schreibt	schrieb	hat geschrieben	write
	schweigen	schweigt	schwieg	hat geschwiegen	be silent
	schwimmen	schwimmt	schwamm	**ist** geschwommen	swim
	sehen	sieht	sah	hat gesehen	see
	sein	**ist**	war	**ist** gewesen	be
	senden	sendet	sandte	hat gesendet	send
	singen	singt	sang	hat gesungen	sing
	sitzen	sitzt	saß	hat(ist) gesessen	sit
	sprechen	spricht	sprach	hat gesprochen	speak, talk
	springen	springt	sprang	**ist** gesprungen	jump
	(statt)finden	findet statt	fand statt	hat stattgefunden	take place
	stehen	steht	stand	hat(ist) gestanden stand	
	steigen	steigt	stieg	**ist** gestiegen	rise, climb
	sterben	stirbt	starb	**ist** gestorben	die
	stoßen	stößt	stieß	hat gestoßen	push
T	**tragen**	trägt	trug	hat getragen	carry, wear
	treffen	trifft	traf	hat getroffen	meet
	trinken	trinkt	trank	hat getrunken	drink
	tun	tut	tat	hat getan	do
U	**umsehen**	sieht sich um	sah sich um	hat sich umgesehen	look round
	umziehen	zieht sich um	zog sich um	hat sich umgezogen	get changed
	umziehen	zieht um	zog um	ist umgezogen	move house
V	**verbinden**	verbindet	verband	hat verbunden	connect, bandage
	verbringen	verbringt	verbrachte	hat verbracht	spend (time)
	vergeben	vergibt	vergab	hat vergeben	forgive
	vergessen	vergißt	vergaß	hat vergessen	forget
	verlassen	verläßt	verließ	hat verlassen	leave (a place)
	verlieren	verliert	verlor	hat verloren	loose
	verschreiben	verschreibt	verschrieb	hat verschrieben	prescribe
	versprechen	verspricht	versprach	hat versprochen	promise
	verstehen	versteht	verstand	hat verstanden	understand
	vertragen	verträgt	vertrug	hat vertragen	bear, stand
	verzeihen	verzeiht	verzieh	hat verziehen	forgive
W	**wachsen**	wächst	wuchs	**ist** gewachsen	grow
	waschen	wäscht (sich)	wusch (sich	hat (sich) gewaschen	wash
	werden	**wird**	wurde	**ist** (ge)worden	become
	werfen	wirft	warf	hat geworfen	throw
	wissen	**weiß**	wußte	hat gewußt	know
	wollen	**will**	wollte	hat gewollt (hat wollen)	want

ADDITIONAL INTERACTIVE ORAL PRACTICE AND GRAMMAR EXERCISES

based on the illustrations 'A German Town', 'A German Landscape' and 'Hotel Zentrum'

- Communication is all here, grammar is of secondary importance. A few incorrect articles or endings don't matter, your tutor will help if necessary.
- Work in pairs or groups, jot down your ideas for the part you are going to take e.g. some questions or answers.
- Short sentences are what you are aiming for in the first instance. More complex structures will gradually evolve as you gain more confidence.

ORAL EXERCISES

based on the illustrations 'A German Town', 'A German Landscape' and 'Hotel Zentrum'

Some examples: Pretend you are one of the people in one of the pictures, can you guess what they want to say?

Jot down a few short sentences, put your notes aside and looking at the illustration say what you think the person might be saying.

This approach can be used very successfully in class where conversations can be practised between two or more students. Unstructured oral practice like this often produces a great deal of hilarity which helps to maintain a pleasant atmosphere.

Topic/situational practice

One can target specific topic areas (e.g. coping with a task in a restaurant, in the bank, checking in at a hotel etc.) asking questions and giving explanations using vocabulary and phrases from the respective chapters or sections in the appendix relevant to the situations depicted . Below are some examples.

Prepare dialogues or decide (with two or more students) which part to take.

Pretend you are:	**participants in the conversation**
ordering food from the waiter	customer/waiter
going shopping in the market	customer/stallholder
going shopping in a store	customer/shop assistant
making a phone-call	student/friend/parents
going to the bank	student/bank clerk
asking the way	student/passer by
getting tickets for trams, trains etc.	student at a kiosk/ticket counter
going to the chemist/drugstore	student/assistant
having trouble with the car	student phoning ADAC, explaining problems, dealing with repair-garage
etc.	

GRAMMAR EXERCISES BASED ON THE ILLUSTRATIONS

'A German Town', 'A German Landscape' and 'Hotel Zentrum'

- The pictures are not only designed to inspire you to speak as much German as possible within the skills areas relevant to the remit of this course but also for practice in all aspects of grammar.
- The examples below are a pointer to the various ways in which the pictures can be used. There are very many ways these pictures can work for the student. Can you think of more ways to exploit the illustrations to make them work for you?

Hier ist ein.................................... ....
eine.................................. ....
[Adj.] [Noun]

Vocabulary, genders, subject case with/without adjectives

Wir sehen einen ....
eine ....
ein ....

Accusative

Was sehen Sie noch ? Viele ....
Grosse ....
Schöne ....

Plurals

Wo ist/sind.....? Das Auto steht neben dem Bus.
Viele Leute sitzen in der Straßenbahn.
Ein junger Mann sitzt auf der Bank.

Dative, prepositions

Was macht/machen....?	Present tense practice Main clause word order Cases
Was haben die Leute vorher gemacht?	Past tenses, main clause word order
Warum?	Subordinate word order*
Was werden die Leute später machen?	Future tense
Warum?	Subordinate word order*

* Don't be afraid to start sentences with 'weil'.

Exercises and vocabulary on the following pages

Exercises: Refer to p. 207 for relevant vocabulary and phrases.

Beschreiben Sie was in jedem Zimmer vorgeht:

Wen sieht man auf diesem Bild?

Was tun diese Personen?

Handeln diese Leute richtig?

Würden Sie auch so handeln? Warum nicht?

Hier findet eine Sitzung statt. Wie ist die Atmosphäre?

Können Sie die Situation erklären?

Wie ist die ideale Sekretärin, der ideale Angestellte?

Der ideale Chef, die ideale Chefin?

Welche Person amüsiert Sie am meisten und warum?

Welche Qualitäten haben Sie? (Here is a chance to reinvent yourself.)

Welche Schwächen? (You are allowed to be selective.)
(die Schwäche(n) weakness)

beschreiben	to describe
vorgehen(s.)	to happen
tun	to do
sehen	to see (er, sie, es sieht)
handeln	to act
stattfinden(s.)	to take place
erklären	to explain

Qualitäten:	**pflichtbewußt**	conscientious	**Schwächen:**	**nachläßig**	negligent
	pünktlich	punctual		**unpünktlich**	unpunctual
	fleißig	hard-working		**faul**	lazy
	verläßlich	reliable		**unverläßlich**	unreliable
	tolerant	tolerant		**intolerant**	intolerant
	geduldig	patient		**ungeduldig**	impatient
	diskret	discrete		**indiskret**	indiscrete
	höflich	polite		**unhöflich**	impolite
	angenehm	pleasant		**unangenehm**	unpleasant
	freundlich	friendly, pleasant		**unfreundlich**	unfriendly
	gepflegt	well turned out		**ungepflegt**	tatty
	sauber	clean		**unsauber**	unclean
	intelligent	intelligent		**unintelligent**	unintelligent
	gescheit	knowledgable		**dumm**	stupid
	klug	clever		**launisch**	moody
	lustig	funny		**langweilig**	boring

das Büro(s)	office
die Firma(en)	company
der Chef(s)	boss (male)
die Chefin(nen)	boss(female)
der Manager(-)	manager
(see also p.170)	
der Besucher(-)	visitor
die Sekretärin(nen)	secretary
der/die Angestellte(n)	employee
der Fensterputzer(-)	window cleaner
der Raumpfleger(-)	cleaner
die Putzfrau(en)	cleaner lady
der Servierwagen	trolley
der Getränkeautomat(en)	drinks machine
das Telefon(e)	telephone
der Beantworter(-)	answering machine
der Computer(-)	computer
die Faxmaschine(n)	fax
die Kopiermaschine(n)	photo copier
der Schreibtisch(e)	writing desk
der Stuhl	chair
der Tisch(e)	table
der Schrank(¨e)	cupboard
das Bücherregal(e)	book shelf
der Aktenschrank(¨e)	filing cabinet
das Fach(¨er)	pigeon hole
das Fenster(-)	window
die Tür(en)	door
der Fußboden(¨en)	floor
die Wand(¨e)	wall
der Korridor(e)	corridor
die Ecke(n)	corner
der Teppich(e)	carpet
der Papierkorb(¨e)	waste-paper basket
die Lampe(n)	lamp
das Papier(e)	paper
die Zeitung(en)	newspaper
die Akte(n)	file
der Aktenordner(-)	file holder
das Buch(¨er)	book
die Mappe(n)	folder
das Dokument(e)	document
der Brief(e)	letter
der Kugelschreiber(-)	biro
(der Kuli)	
der Füller(-)	pen
(die Füllfeder)	
der Blei(s)	pencil
(der Bleistift)	
der Farbstift(e)	colour pencil
der Filzstift(e)	felt pen

eine Sitzung (Besprechung) haben
to have a meeting

böse sein	to be cross
sprechen	to speak, talk
zeigen	to show
(zeigen auf	to point)
warten	to wait
lesen	to read
die Nägel lackieren	to paint one's nails
essen, trinken	to eat, drink
gähnen	to yawn
putzen	to clean (also 'reinigen')
lächeln	to smile
Kaffee/Tee anbieten	to offer coffee/tea
arbeiten	to work
telefonieren	to phone
(be)antworten	to answer
am Computer arbeiten	to work at the computer
faxen	to fax
kopieren	to copy
schreiben	to write
sitzen	to sit
stehen	to stand
liegen	to lie
sehen	to see

durch das Fenster schauen (gucken)
to look through the window
den Boden reinigen
to clean the floor

tragen	to carry
halten	to hold
übergehen	to overflow
öffnen	to open
schließen	to shut

to put:	**geben**	(+ dat.)
	tun	
	legen	flat objects e.g. paper, book
	stellen	tall objects e.g. bottle, glas
	stecken	into confined spaces like drawers, pockets etc.

BASIC CONCEPT BEHIND 'GERMAN WITH A SMILE'

1
CORE LANGUAGE

for basic level proficiency

Skeleton grammar only, situational (topic related) basic vocabulary + phrases, highlighted in bold throughout the text and emphasis on speaking.

Core language of all topics, chapter by chapter, will enable you to gain overall practical knowledge. Concentrating on a selection of topics only will build up the language in a modular fashion, as you need it.

2
COMPLETE COURSE

for intermediate level competence

Made up of the core language plus the rest of the course material up to chapter 16, extended by a useful reference section and grammar survey.

additional structures
+
⇧
add. oral work + ⇦ **Core Language** ⇨ + add. topic work
⇩
+
additonal grammar

3
APPENDIX

Very useful reference material considerably extending the scope of this book with a wealth of supplementary information

---

4
GRAMMAR SURVEY

Presenting all the essentials of grammar in a logical progression, to be dipped into when necessary.

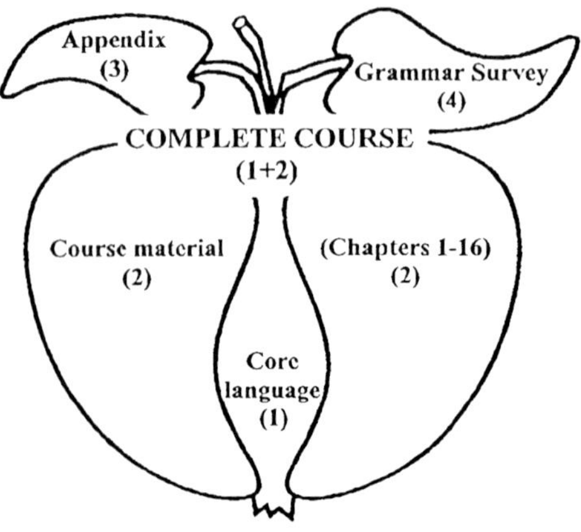

All the language work is carefully graded to give you a gently rising learning curve. Although all the course components are inter-connected they also lend themselves to be used separately in a modular fashion.

Available from all good booksellers or direct from the publishers

Coach House Publications
The Old Coach House
School Green Lane
Freshwater
Isle of Wight
PO40 9BB

Tel/Fax: 01983 755655

FRÜHER · EARLIER ON

GRANDCHILDREN

DER ENKEL · DIE ENKELIN